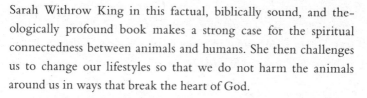
Sarah Withrow King in this factual, biblically sound, and theologically profound book makes a strong case for the spiritual connectedness between animals and humans. She then challenges us to change our lifestyles so that we do not harm the animals around us in ways that break the heart of God.

—Tony Campolo, PhD, Professor Emeritus, Eastern University

This book signals the end of an era in which the Bible has been selectively and erroneously used to justify how the world thinks about animals. A very diverse group of theologians and biblical scholars have been challenging this received wisdom in recent years, but King expertly connects their ideas to a much broader audience. Anyone who takes the Bible seriously as God's Word will find themselves deeply challenged—and perhaps even brought closer to God—by wrestling with this book.

—Charles Camosy, Associate Professor
of Theology, Fordham University

In her eminently readable *Vegangelical*, Sarah Withrow King combines wry personal testimony, evangelical reflection upon Scripture, and bracing accounts of contemporary treatment of animals. The result is an inviting yet prophetic challenge that should be faithfully considered not only by all Christian animal lovers but by all who believe God is love.

—William Greenway, Associate Professor of Philosophical
Theology, Austin Presbyterian Theological Seminary; author,
For the Love of All Creatures: The Story of Grace in Genesis

I'm grateful for my friend Sarah Withrow King and this important book she has written. God cares for his creation and made us in his image so we could too. Although it has often been a blind spot in our churches, how we treat God's other (nonhuman) creatures is integral to our discipleship and witness today. It also has serious implications for the health of both people and the planet. These aren't easy questions—and they may have more than one answer—but they're important and biblical ones that need asking. And Sarah is an honest and thoughtful guide for all of us committed to living more faithfully in a world too full of violence and suffering.

—**Rev. Ben Lowe,** activist; author, *Doing Good without Giving Up* and *The Future of Our Faith*

This book will open your eyes to truths that will make you a better human being. Your understanding of compassion, violence, and life will be transformed.

—**Rev. Carlos L. Malavé,** Executive Director, Christian Churches Together

Sarah Withrow King offers a thoughtful invitation to Christians to consider our relationship with animals in light of our faith. *Vegangelical* is an articulate, sincere introduction to Bible-based social and environmental justice, opening the conversation to how God forms us through our interactions with the created world. A must-read for protectors of all creatures, great and small.

—**Nancy Sleeth,** cofounder, Blessed Earth

A significant introduction to the important but too-long neglected topic of a solidly Christian approach to the (mis)treatment of animals. One need not agree with every argument to realize this book presents an urgent challenge that biblical Christians dare no longer ignore. King's chilling stories, extensive statistics, and probing biblical arguments offer a great place to begin.

—**Ronald J. Sider,** Senior Distinguished Professor of Theology, Holistic Ministry, and Public Policy, Palmer Seminary at Eastern University

Vegangelical

Vegangelical

*How Caring for Animals
Can Shape Your Faith*

Sarah Withrow King

 ZONDERVAN®

241.6
KIN

ZONDERVAN

Vegangelical
Copyright © 2016 by Sarah Withrow King

This title is also available as a Zondervan ebook.
Visit www.zondervan.com/ebooks.

Requests for information should be addressed to:
Zondervan, 3900 Sparks Dr. SE, Grand Rapids, Michigan 49546

Library of Congress Cataloging-in-Publication Data

Names: King, Sarah Withrow, 1978- author.
Title: Vegangelical : how caring for animals can shape your faith / Sarah
   Withrow King.
Description: Grand Rapids : Zondervan, 2016. | Includes bibliographical
   references.
Identifiers: LCCN 2015047337 | ISBN 9780310522379 (softcover)
Subjects: LCSH: Animals — Religious aspects — Christianity. | Animal welfare —
   Religious aspects — Christianity.
Classification: LCC BT746 .K565 2016 | DDC 241/.693 — dc23 LC record available
   at http://lccn.loc.gov/2015047337

Cover design: Rocket Republic
Cover art: Shutterstock
Interior imagery: PhotoDisc
Interior design: Kait Lamphere

Printed in the United States of America

16 17 18 19 20 21 22 23 24 25 /DHV/ 15 14 13 12 11 10 9 8 7 6 5 4 3 2 1

To Mom and Dad:
Thank you for showing me how to follow Jesus.

To Giehl:
Thank you for clearing the path.

And to Isaiah:
Thank you for reminding me every day of the
promise that one day the lion and the lamb will lie
down together and a little child shall lead them.

Contents

Acknowledgments

Writing this book felt a lot like being pregnant. It disrupted and changed the course of my life, brought on worries about things that were entirely out of my control, and was suddenly over after nine months of sleepless nights. And just as pregnancy, birth, and the mind-bogglingly difficult task of child-rearing are made a bit easier when they are steeped in community, so my community gave my family the love and support we needed to birth this book.

Mae Cannon believed I had something important to say and was my champion and advocate. Madison Trammel at Zondervan managed to both sharpen and encourage with his feedback on my early ideas and the manuscript. Nicole Morgan did an excellent job doing research for and providing feedback on early drafts; her input helped shape the structure of the book in important ways.

I am indebted to the theologians and writers who have been working out these issues for decades, especially Andrew Linzey, David Clough, and Richard Bauckham. Any shortcomings in my analysis are my mistakes, not theirs. I am grateful for the faculty of Palmer Seminary, who shepherded me through a master's degree in theology with extraordinary skill, exposing me to a diverse range of thinkers and theologians who have shaped not only my writing but my faith.

Our church community, Circle of Hope, helped fill gaps that I left when I retreated to my room to write by hosting my family, meeting my son at the bus stop when I couldn't, and urging me to get out of the house at least once every week or so. Beth invited me to exercise, which cleared my head at just the right times, and reminded me over and over that I was capable and strong.

And Giehl and Isaiah. My boys. I love you both and thank you for the freedom to pursue this important work. I'll make dinner tonight.

Introduction

Why Me? and Why This Book?

I'm a Christian and an animal advocate, so I almost never get invited to dinner parties. Inevitably I'll end up talking about Jesus or chickens; also, I know only the worst jokes and am really bad at small talk.

I never thought this was where I'd land—living in a row house in Philadelphia, a seminary degree under my nonleather belt, working full-time for animal protection. When my freshman-year college advisor asked me what I wanted to do, I told him I wanted to run a bed-and-breakfast along the Oregon coast. He pointed out I didn't need a degree for that, so I spent the next six years bouncing from college to college, major to major, mission to mission. I wanted desperately to know that I was doing God's will, making a difference, being a faithful servant.

My parents met and married shortly after becoming Christians in the mid-1970s in Boise, Idaho. I was born into their faith and raised on community, service, and religious dialogue. We read and discussed the Scriptures as a family, and I was encouraged to develop a personal relationship with Jesus Christ. I was baptized at ten years old, went to church camp and youth group, listened to bands like Point of Grace and Petra, took a purity oath, and tried really hard to read my Bible every day. As I matured, my parents trusted me with freedom, and I used it wisely—most of the time. I remain deeply grateful to my parents for their wisdom. I hope my husband and I are able to instill in our son the same yearning for and trust in Christ that my parents showed me.

I've always had a passion for justice. A strong sense of right and wrong. A feeling of solidarity with those who are powerless, bullied, or abused. I thought I could be a lawyer for International Justice Mission, a doctor without borders, a member of the Peace Corps, an equalizer of public education funding, or an activist for the unborn. Though I felt relatively helpless to make a significant impact on the world, the calling to be a friend of and advocate for the marginalized has always been deeply entwined with my faith. Yes, we're justified by faith alone, but our praxis—how we live, how we practice our faith—is an important part of how we deepen that faith and share it with others.

In my early twenties, I went to lunch with my brother and picked up a booklet that changed the course of my life. The tract described the mutilation and abuse suffered by animals raised and killed for food. I read for the first time about the gross resource inefficiency of land, water, and grain in raising animals for food and that there was a direct connection between the meat I ate and someone else's going hungry. I read also about the health benefits of plant-based diets, that they lower choles-terol and dramatically decrease the risk of cancer, heart disease, stroke, diabetes, and other life-threatening conditions.

I was first horrified, then angry, then determined and empowered.

I stopped eating animals. Then I stopped buying products that were tested on animals and clothes that were made of ani-mal skins. It was a gradual process.

When I finally graduated college with a degree in political science, a newfound knowledge of the human use of animals, and the ever-present desire to serve, I applied for a job at People for the Ethical Treatment of Animals (PETA). I knew very little about the organization when I began work there in November 2002, except that it existed and that the motto "Animals are not ours to eat, wear, experiment on, or use for entertainment" resonated with me on a deep level.

For nine years, I grew in faith as I grew in knowledge of the horrific ways and endless justifications humans have concocted to use and abuse animals. While a few of my church friends seemed to get it, most of the folks I worshiped with were bemused by, annoyed with, or downright angry at my convictions. And during the workdays, I talked to countless young people who had left the church because of the hypocrisy they perceived in followers of the Prince of Peace, the God of love, who appeared indifferent to the massive scale of suffering endured by God's created beings at the hands of humans.

I held these two parts of my life apart from each other for a very long time, perhaps because I am slow and thickheaded. Happily, God is patient and creative.

I was sitting in worship one Sunday morning, watching a short video in which music and cool graphics are put to Scripture. The words were from Isaiah, about sacrifice and blood, and as I read them, I found myself thinking, "This would be so powerful with video from factory farms and slaughterhouses behind the words." Then shortly thereafter, "Sarah, you're the only one in this room of hundreds who is having that thought."

Then God spoke. It was a response like we sometimes hear in prayer when we're able to quiet our hearts and listen for God's leading. I finally understood that there was a purpose for my passion for Jesus and animals. And my next step became crystal clear: seminary. God was calling me to learn more, to build bridges, and to live into the calling placed on my heart.

My husband and I started to look at seminaries, and we met with the senior pastor at our church to get his blessing. During that meeting, Pastor Jim asked if I'd ever read *Rich Christians in an Age of Hunger* by Ron Sider and suggested that I take a look at Palmer Theological Seminary, where Sider taught.

Palmer was in Philadelphia and my husband and I were in Norfolk, Virginia, but God made a way out of no way, and I started classes at Palmer in 2011. I quit my job at PETA because I was commuting and had a scholarship that required me to work for The Sider Center. My first project with the center was to research the environmental impacts of animal agriculture for a chapter one of my professors was writing on the ethics of eating meat. I was home.

For the next three years as I worked toward a master of theological studies degree, I focused on questions surrounding Christianity and animals. Nearly every paper I wrote explored the theological foundation for and practical implications of "animal rights," and when I graduated in May 2014, it was with a depth and breadth of knowledge I'd never imagined possible, along with the humbling awareness there was still much to learn.

Before seminary, I felt conflicted about whether and how my faith really required compassion for animals. I questioned whether my attachment to the ethic of animal care was sentimental rather than biblical.

What I learned is that the church has a rich history of animal protection, and just as the Israelites were "blessed to be a blessing," so all people, made in the image of God, are blessed to bless, not to oppress. I realized being a Jesus follower means giving special consideration to those who are most vulnerable, and being vegan is a natural and good expression of God's grace, mercy, and justice. I call myself and this book "Vegangelical" because caring for animals has helped me appreciate the Good News in deeper and wider ways, and though the work is often heartbreaking, I have hope in a resurrected Christ, who is calling his whole creation home.

Why Me?

Perhaps you've noticed that vegans get tossed onto desert islands and into postapocalyptic survival scenarios more, I think, than the average Josephine.

> "Okay, I get why you don't want to eat meat *now*, but if you were stranded on a desert island and had to eat meat to survive, would you?"
> "What if it were just you and a dog in a lifeboat, but it could only hold one of you? Who would you save?"
> "But if you were being attacked by a bear, you'd kill it, right?"

And then there are the more practical what-ifs:

> "What if I shot a deer who'd lived its entire life happily in the forest and died instantly; would you eat it?"
> "What if the chicken/cow/pig had a truly happy life and a quick death; would you eat it?"
> "What if the chicken/cow/pig had a truly happy life and a quick death; would it be wrong to eat it?"
> "What if testing on animals saves human lives? Isn't that good?"

Animal welfarists, when pressed on the second set of questions, will answer that it's ethical to eat animals if they have happy lives and painless deaths, and it's ethical to use them for testing and other means if there is a clear benefit to humans and the animals are treated as well as possible. Most people can claim support for animal welfare. I don't think that's good enough for Christians, though, and especially not Christians who live in affluence relative to the rest of the globe. I'll challenge you, dear reader, to stick with me even if this initial confession makes you feel angry or annoyed or argumentative.

I was in Nicaragua once, working with a small team to install a pump and water-filtration system in a small community's well and to teach residents about clean-water use and hygiene. We stayed in a home built by hand out of clay and wood, with a corrugated tin roof and a sturdy outhouse. The family kept chickens who freely roamed the small property. One cool night, a mama and her chicks slept underneath one of our cots, cooing back and forth to one another. At dinner the second night we were there, parts of a chicken showed up on the plate I was served for dinner. Not wanting to insult our hostess and the incredible efforts she and her daughters had made to cook for three additional people, I considered just eating what I was served. But I looked at the other food on my plate: sliced and fried potatoes, black beans and tomatoes smothered with fresh avocado, and tortillas that I heard Rosa rise to make every day at 4:00 a.m., and I realized that I didn't need the chicken to sustain myself. Our translator and one of my teammates quietly split the meat between them. We explained the next morning that I didn't eat meat, and I wasn't served flesh again. I got extra avocado, which didn't make me a bit sad!

I looked. I realized. I didn't need.

Why This Book?

While secular thinkers have produced a large volume of literature on the human-animal relationship, only a few Jesus followers have taken up the subject seriously. As a result, even though animals are an integral part of everyday life for most Christians, we have little, if any, theological framework to govern our treatment of animals. This leaves Christians without a biblical approach to issues like factory farming, animal experimentation, and so on. But in a world where it takes sixteen pounds of grain to produce a single pound of beef, where the toxins from factory farms pollute communities and sicken workers, and where

God-created species are disappearing from the face of the planet, these issues simply can't be ignored.

This book is for Christians who are curious about what "animal rights" is all about and why it matters. It's a contribution to a larger body of theology about who we are as humans and how we ought to live in the world. It will cover much but also will leave much unsaid. I hope this book gets you thinking in new ways. At some points, the changes I suggest to our thinking and actions may seem daunting and personal. I'll ask questions, and I hope you will prayerfully consider them and resist what may be a strong temptation to take a defensive posture. I've been having conversations about humans, animals, and God for more than a decade, and I'm still inquiring, discovering, wrestling. There will be many opportunities in these pages for you to do the same.

As I've journeyed along this road, a few theological concepts have come up again and again that I've found particularly helpful in developing a Christian animal ethic: *imago Dei*, dominion and stewardship, and love. I'll talk about each of these in the coming chapters, along with service, worship, and grace. After exploring this theological foundation, I will look at how humans are using animals today, as companions and entertainment and for research, food, and clothing. In the conclusion, I'll offer practical guidance for readers who want to start making changes in their lives to alleviate animal suffering.

Let's get started, shall we?

PART 1

Theological Foundation

Over and over, God has spoken to me through the Bible. The Scriptures confound my expectations, challenge me to change, instruct me to pause, and inspire me to press on. I have a tendency toward depression, but the arc of the biblical story is one of hope, and I am reminded of that each time I open its pages. The Bible shows us how to live as the community of God's creation, presents the gift of stories from our spiritual ancestors, and points us toward reconciliation with one another and with God.

But the Bible doesn't directly address all situations through all time. We can't open this book and know if we should vote for one candidate or another in the US presidential election. There is no verse that tells us how to respond when the head of a foreign government uses chemical weapons on his own citizens. The Bible doesn't dictate what kind of car we should drive, which career we should pursue, or whether we should send our kids to private school or to the struggling public school around the corner.

As a Jesus follower, I want to live in a way that honors and reflects Jesus. I want to do God's will. God gives us spiritual leaders, a community of believers, and prayer to help light our way. And we have the Bible, a canon of divinely inspired writings, God breathed, through which we can hear God's voice.

Ron Sider has been examining and guiding evangelical political engagement for longer than I have been alive. His hunger to follow Jesus and to ground his life and work in biblical principles is evident to anyone who knows him. Long ago, Sider developed a methodology for examining political choices that I have adapted to my work as well.[1]

There are political issues at work in human-animal relationships, of course. Agriculture in the United States is a huge and influential industry. Voters are asked regularly to weigh in on ballot measures that affect animal welfare. While these issues will not be the focus of this book, the methodology still applies to the everyday choices we make that, in ways big and small, impact the world around us.

First, Sider suggests that Christians go to Scripture to develop a normative framework that can serve as a lens through which specific issues can be examined. Such a framework is formed by properly examining and exegeting the whole canon of Scripture to gain "a biblical view of the world and persons that flows from the biblical story."[2] The second stage of Sider's analysis is to carry out a study of the world. The third step is to develop a political philosophy, and fourth is to conduct a detailed social analysis of political issues.

In my modification of Sider's methodology, I combine the second and fourth steps and eliminate the third. So this book will establish a biblical foundation for our thoughts and actions as Christians, then look at what is happening in the world. The final step is up to you: to choose to act in the world in ways that reflect biblical values.

I want desperately to tell you what I know about how humans use animals today. The facts are shocking, and they are daily realities for billions of God's sentient creatures all around the globe. I'll do that in the second part of the book. The truth doesn't need to be embellished; on its face, the way we treat animals today is astonishingly cruel.

It's important that you know a bit about me and the premises from which I'm starting before we embark on this journey, so you know what motivates me to act on behalf of animals. I was a Christian long before I was a vegan or an animal advocate, and my faith in Christ and the hope of reconciliation are what keep me trodding on this often sorrowful path. I believe that God is Lord of all and that Jesus is God enfleshed. I believe that Jesus inaugurated the kingdom of God on earth and that this kingdom is marked by the triumph of life over death, as evidenced by the death and resurrection of Christ and by the reconciliation of creation back to the Creator. I also believe that the very nature of God—the Trinitarian God in and through whom *all* life flows—points us to a way of living in the world that requires humility, interdependence, transformation, and love beyond what is comfortable.

A number of biblical principles can help us develop a normative framework for our relationship with animals. I've chosen to focus on three.

1. *Imago Dei:* What does it mean to be made in the image of a Trinitarian God, and how ought that inform our treatment of animals?
2. *Dominion and stewardship:* What does it mean to steward creation, and are stewardship and dominion compatible?
3. *The "other":* How are we called to extend mercy to "the least of these," and who is our neighbor?

I chose these three because they are foundational in the development of a whole-life ethic. How we see ourselves, and especially how we see ourselves in relation to God and to one another, informs every decision we make.

Whenever I talk about being a Christian vegan, someone inevitably brings up Peter's vision in Acts 10. ("Get up, Peter. Kill and eat.") Yet what folks often miss is the surrounding passage and the point of the vision: God is telling Peter to extend far beyond his comfort zone, to take the good news of Christ to the "other."

One of our challenges as Jesus followers is to look around and identify what we are doing that pushes others to the margins, creates an "us" and a "them," and denies love, justice, and righteousness. If we think carefully, honestly, and prayerfully about how being made in the image of a Trinitarian God ought to inform our exercise of stewardship and dominion over those who are most different from us, I think we might find ourselves quite as astonished as Peter at what we hear.

CHAPTER 1

Made in the Image of the Trinitarian God

Imaging God, Despite Ourselves

The Son is the image of the invisible God, the firstborn over all creation. For in him all things were created: things in heaven and on earth, visible and invisible, whether thrones or powers or rulers or authorities; all things have been created through him and for him. He is before all things, and in him all things hold together. . . . For God was pleased to have all his fullness dwell in him, and through him to reconcile to himself all things, whether things on earth or things in heaven, by making peace through his blood, shed on the cross.

—*Colossians 1:15–17, 19–20*

Here is what greeted me one morning in my Facebook news feed:

- A new post announced the birth of a long-awaited baby boy.
- A ninety-five-year-old WWII veteran was shot and killed by a police officer who felt the elderly man was a threat to the officer's safety.
- ISIS members pushed two men "convicted" of being gay off an eight-story building.

- The manager of a Subway restaurant gives a homeless man a sandwich every evening in exchange for sweeping and mopping the floors, then drives him to a shelter.
- A Wall Street executive quit his job to open a pizzeria where each slice costs a dollar, and if you give an extra dollar, a homeless person can come claim a free slice.
- A Texas company is auctioning off the chance to kill rare species of animals in a series of "canned hunts."
- A heartbreaking video shows a little boy, distraught over a dead fish found washed up on a beach, holding and caressing the fish, trying to bring her back to life.
- A new report found that half the schoolchildren in America live below the poverty line.
- A fourteen-year-old boy stabbed in the chest last night in West Philadelphia has died.
- Thousands have been killed in Nigeria, slaughtered at the hand of religious extremists.

Victims and celebrants and killers and mourners united by the confounding, sometimes maddening fact that all are made in the image of God.

For those who care, it can seem like a heavy burden to bear. I am made in the image of God. God! Me! I'm hardly up for the task. I sleep too late, snipe at my husband, complain about loud music coming from a car parked in the street, don't call my mother enough, follow my stomach too much, forget to stash cash and food in my purse for panhandlers, isolate myself, swear, am judgmental and controlling, and tend to wallow in self-pity, anxiety, and shame. When I was in middle school, I told a group of my peers that I thought we should put "all the gays on an island and blow it up." In high school, I told the one African American boy in my class that racism was "over." I was made in the image of God then too, but I have a hard time accepting that now.

And yet.

When I'm able to come to terms with the fact that I(mperfect) am made in the image of God, I still must grapple with the reality that so are the people whom I find it so difficult to love. The boy who called me "thunder thighs" while we were waiting for the bus in middle school. The neighbor who screams at her toddler in the pharmacy waiting area. The distant relative who blames the president for the demise of America and makes every family gathering an exercise in verbal restraint. The people who wield guns and walk into malls, movie theaters, and schools to kill dozens upon dozens of other people. The farm supervisor who rams a cane into a pig's vagina, then brags about it. All these too are made in the image of God.

Inexplicable? Perhaps. If we are to understand what it means to be made in the image of God, we first should discover who God is.

Who Is God?

Dear friends, let us love one another, for love comes from God. Everyone who loves has been born of God and knows God. Whoever does not love does not know God, because God is love. This is how God showed his love among us: He sent his one and only Son into the world that we might live through him. This is love: not that we loved God, but that he loved us and sent his Son as an atoning sacrifice for our sins. Dear friends, since God so loved us, we also ought to love one another. No one has ever seen God; but if we love one another, God lives in us and his love is made complete in us.

—1 John 4:7–12

Some things in life are important to complexify. When I look at readily available cheap food or a great sale, I think it's important to ask, "Why?" and, "Whose sacrifice made this possible?" Why can I get a car loan, a credit card, or a job relatively easily, when my neighbors struggle? Why can my husband walk our son to school without getting harassed by neighborhood police, but the same isn't true for my friend who lives in a "nicer" part of town and whose husband has darker skin than mine? Complicated questions require more than soundbite answers.

But when I ask, "Who is God?" again and again, the answer is clear and simple: God is love. God *is* and the *is* is love. Beloved, let us love one another because God is love. Now, God is also angry sometimes and jealous. God wants obedience, and we frequently fail to deliver. Does that lessen love? Not in the least. Parents know that anger, disappointment, even fury can all be felt alongside and in the midst of love. God is all this and God is love.

The reality of this life makes it easy to muddy these waters: If God is love, why do bad things happen? If God is love, why is there so much evil in the world? If God is love, why do tsunamis and tornadoes kill indiscriminately? If God is love, why did my baby son die? If God is love, why does he seem to ignore me in my darkest hour, when depression has clenched my heart and mind? If God is love, why did my wife die a slow death from a degenerative disease? If God is love, why did my father hit me, and my mother leave? If God is love, why can't I stop eating until I feel sick? If God is love, why are God's followers so awful, so often?

Friends of mine who grew up in the church and who have left sometimes call the God they grew up knowing "misogynist" and "murderer." Those who have come to care about nonhuman creation could add "animal abuser" to that list. They read the Bible as a tale of tragedy, with God a dispassionate and distant observer, content to watch all creation descend into chaos, to fiddle while the planet burns.

And yet, as hard as it is to live in this broken world, *this* is the reality that no amount of evil can change: God is love. And the world God made is good.

The light is good (Gen. 1:4); the waters and the dry land are good (v. 10); the vegetation brought forth by the earth through God's word is good (v. 12); the sun and the moon, day and night are good (vv. 17–18); every living creature in the water and in the sky is good (v. 21) and blessed (v. 22); every living creature of the land is good (v. 25). Everything God makes is very good (v. 31).

It's easy, I think, to get caught up in the lie that "worm theology" wants us to live in, the lie that says we children of God are undesirable, miserable beings, good for nothing and destined for anguish, suffering, and pain. But the Bible tells a very different story. We are beloved.

From Love and Goodness, God Creates and Sustains

In the beginning was the Word, and the Word was with God, and the Word was God. He was with God in the beginning. Through him all things were made; without him nothing was made that has been made.

—*John 1:1–3*

How do we *know* that God is love? Scripture first shows us God's love in creation and then in Jesus. German theologian Jürgen Moltmann says, "[God's] self-communicating love for the one like himself [Jesus] opens itself to the Other and becomes creative . . . [B]ecause he creates the world by virtue of his eternal love for the Son, the world is, through his eternal will, destined for good, and is nothing other than an expression of his love. The world is good, just as God is himself goodness."[1] God's love is so expansive that worlds, planets, stars, the sun, the moon, *all life* flows out of, into, and through God. God's love is life creating, life sustaining, and life saving.

The Hebrew word used in Genesis 1 for "good" (*tov*) is found hundreds of times in the Old Testament. It is a life-generating goodness, instructive for us as we consider how we conceive of the love of God.[2] In the following passages, I have substituted "life-generating" or a similar word or phrase for "good" (*tov*). Consider how the alternate wording might affect how we are called to respond to God's love.

As an exiled people return home and begin to rebuild the temple, they celebrate the laying of the foundation. "With praise and thanksgiving they sang to the LORD: 'He is [life-generating]; his love toward Israel endures forever'" (Ezra 3:11).

David knew that God brought goodness in the midst of strife: "Many, LORD, are asking, 'Who will bring us [life]?' Let the light of your face shine on us!" (Ps. 4:6). God is more than a shepherd simply watching over a flock. The flock is of God, created from the words and hands, from the very being, of God. As a result, "surely [the generation of life] and love will follow me all the days of my life, and I will dwell in the house of the LORD forever" (Ps. 23:6).

This is a Creator God who is deeply invested in the creative work. "[Life-generating] and upright is the LORD; therefore he instructs sinners in his ways. He guides the humble in what is right and teaches them his way. All the ways of the LORD are loving and faithful toward those who keep the demands of his covenant" (Ps. 25:8–10).

This is a Sustainer God who is an active, continually generating presence in the world: "The LORD is [life-generating] to those whose hope is in him, to the one who seeks him" (Lam. 3:25).

God so loves the whole creation, in fact, that God takes on the vulnerable flesh of a creaturely being and inserts himself as the infant son of an unwed Jewish girl living under the tyrannical occupation of one of history's most terrible armies. And this, too, is good. "How beautiful on the mountains are the feet of those who bring [life-generating] news, who proclaim peace, who bring good tidings, who proclaim salvation, who say to Zion, 'Your God reigns!'" (Isa. 52:7).

As a product of God's loving creation, we also are capable of and called to goodness. "Seek [the generation of life], not evil, that you may live. Then the LORD God Almighty will be with you, just as you say he is. Hate evil, love [life]; maintain justice in the courts. Perhaps the LORD God Almighty will have mercy on the remnant of Joseph" (Amos 5:14–15).

This is not just a private good, a quiet piety. The goodness to which we are called extends into the public sphere, permeating the spaces in which we walk, learn, and live. This goodness is active. "He has shown you, O mortal, what is [life-generating]. And what does the LORD require of you? To act justly and to love mercy[3] and to walk humbly with your God" (Mic. 6:8). Because to love must also mean to seek righteousness. "Anyone who does not do what is right is not God's child, nor is anyone who does not love their brother and sister" (1 John 3:10).

And what of love?

The Scriptures are full of references to and stories about God's love for creation. Psalm 104 praises God for the majesty and care of creation, describing in loving detail how God gives every animal a drink of water, provides shelter for birds, gladdens human hearts, and provides plants for humans and animals alike to eat. "How many are your works, LORD! In wisdom you made them all; the earth is full of your creatures. There is the sea, vast and spacious, teeming with creatures beyond number— living things both large and small" (vv. 24–25).

God loves this very good world. The Old Testament writers noted this love through God's patience and provision for a hard-headed people through centuries of war, famine, disobedience, abundance, exile, and more. The New Testament writers noted this love through the life and death of Jesus. And though grace is a gift, freely given, Jesus repeatedly calls us to show love to one another as a reflection of God's love for us.

Our Response and Responsibility: To Love

> A new command I give you: Love one another. As I have loved you, so you must love one another. By this everyone will know that you are my disciples, if you love one another.
> —*John 13:34–35*

Ask anyone who has been married more than a couple of years and hopefully they will tell you that love isn't a feeling. Love, particularly the *agape* love so often spoken of in the New Testament, is an active word—a moral preference, what God prefers. Romans 5:8 illustrates this well: "But God demonstrates his own love for us in this: While we were still sinners, Christ died for us." This is not Hallmark Channel love; this is love that is hard and messy and dangerous. Love is to be pursued (1 Cor. 14:1; 1 Tim. 6:11), maintained (1 Peter 4:8), and shared (1 John 3:16).

We are called to *abide* in God's love (1 John 4:7–21), to continue to be present in our love of God and of one another. The two are deeply connected. To love God is to love others. To love others is to love God. In fact, this mutuality is the very nature of the Trinitarian God.

What Does It Mean for God to Be Trinitarian?

> Jesus gave them this answer: "Very truly I tell you, the Son can do nothing by himself; he can do only what he sees his Father doing, because whatever the Father does the Son

also does. For the Father loves the Son and shows him all he does. Yes, and he will show him even greater works than these, so that you will be amazed. For just as the Father raises the dead and gives them life, even so the Son gives life to whom he is pleased to give it."

—*John 5:19–21*

The Greek word that Jesus uses to talk about the love between him and God here is *philei*, meaning a warm affection or intimate friendship, and it is a form of the same word Jesus uses later in John's gospel on the night he was betrayed to describe God's love for his disciples: "The Father himself loves you because you have loved me and have believed that I came from God" (John 16:27). This is the intimacy to which we are called, with both God and one another—and it is this intimacy that is the very essence of the Trinity.

Growing up, I didn't understand the Trinity or see its relevance to everyday life or faith. Friends would ask me how I could believe in three gods but only one God, and I really didn't have a good answer for them. In Sunday school I learned some bad analogies that didn't help me to grasp the complexity of this particular doctrine; for example, that God is like an egg with the yolk, the white, and the shell (one thing with three parts), or that God is like water, ice, and steam (three forms of one substance).

But understanding the Trinity is critical for understanding what it means to image God. And once we do understand, once we dig beneath the surface of our Sunday school theology, we discover that the Trinity is a gift that makes every part of our lives as Jesus followers that much richer, that much more challenging, and that much more beautiful.[4]

Scripture points to the Trinity, but of course there's no explicit reference to it in the Bible. The early church struggled with how to define God and Jesus and the Holy Spirit as "one God." Some early Christians suggested that Jesus wasn't God, but God-like, which didn't sit well with others. When bishops gathered at the Council of Nicaea in the year AD 325, they decided that Jesus and God are of the same substance, in other words, that Christ is fully God. The church wasn't fully united, however. Greek-speaking Christians (precursors to the Orthodox Church) held to the idea that God was made of three particular beings sharing a single essence. Latin-speaking Christians (precursors to the Roman Catholic Church) believed that God was one essence with three persons, or roles. Greeks probably would have appreciated the water/ice/vapor Trinity analogy, while the Latin folks would have been more likely to go with the egg analogy. Subtle, but significant, differences in emphases.

As the centuries have marched on, theologians have continued to struggle with how to talk about God, Jesus, and the Holy Spirit. Theologian William Placher, longtime professor at Wabash College, argued that one of the most important consequences of the ongoing debate is that we are forced to really consider who we believe God is. Some Christians continue to view God as a distant and stern father figure, an old man with a long beard on top of a faraway mountain. Some others think that God *must* remain distant because bending down would be a sign of weakness. Early Greek theologians (with their emphasis on the three-ness of God) "insisted that this reaching down in love is not at all a sign of divine weakness. In fact . . . we learn how *great* God is precisely in God's ability and willingness to come to 'our weak nature.' A God who could not reach out in love would be a lesser God."[5]

A Trinitarian God can't be untouchable, uninterested, or uncaring. Moltmann describes the significance of the Trinity in the best way I've read: "The Father exists in the Son, the Son in the Father, and both of them in the Spirit, just as the Spirit exists in both the Father and the Son. By virtue of their eternal love they live in one another to such an extent . . . that they are one. It is a process of most perfect and intense empathy."[6] This is *perichoresis*, fellowship and intimacy. The Greek and Latin words in translation call up a vision of God stepping toward and around and among God's self in an eternal, holy dance. *Perichoresis* is mutual interdependence, mutual submission. And if we imitate it, we live in community, interdependence, and empathy. Moltmann again: "The Persons of the Trinity make one another shine through that glory, mutually and together. They glow into perfect form through one another and awake to perfected beauty in one another."[7]

There is no room in this relationship, a relationship of mutuality and empathy, for domination or oppression.[8] Some argue that God is a child abuser, sending Jesus to a violent and gruesome death on a cross. But the reality of the Trinitarian God is that it is impossible for one to coerce the other. Jesus, fully God and fully human, freely goes to the cross, freely suffers with and for us, dies, and then conquers death through his resurrection.

A Trinitarian God models relationship, exists *in relationship*. It's why believers also must live *in relationship* with others and resist the urge to isolate ourselves from the pain and struggles of the world, from the irritation and inconvenience that come with being around other imperfect people.

For me, the most poignant illustration of this perichoretic relationship is found in the following two passages from the New Testament: "My prayer is not for them alone. I pray also for those who will believe in me through their message, that all of them may be one, Father, just as you are in me and I am in you. May they also be in us. . . . I have given them the glory that you gave me, that they may be one as we are one—I in them and you in me—so that they may be brought to complete unity.

Then the world will know that you sent me and have loved them even as you have loved me . . . before the creation of the world" (John 17:20–24).

Hours before Jesus is betrayed by Judas, tried by Pilate, denied by Peter, and tortured by Roman soldiers, he prays for his disciples and all who will follow after them. He prays, above all, for unity. He prays that God will draw Jesus' earthly companions to God's self, that they may be one with God and one with each other. This fervent hope was at the forefront of Jesus' mind on the eve of his crucifixion.

A few decades after Christ's death and resurrection, Paul's letter to the Romans expands on this holy desire for unity.

> I consider that our present sufferings are not worth comparing with the glory that will be revealed in us. For the creation waits in eager expectation for the children of God to be revealed. For the creation was subjected to frustration, not by its own choice, but by the will of the one who subjected it, in hope that the creation itself will be liberated from its bondage to decay and brought into the freedom and glory of the children of God.
>
> We know that the whole creation has been groaning as in the pains of childbirth right up to the present time. Not only so, but we ourselves, who have the firstfruits of the Spirit, groan inwardly as we wait eagerly for our adoption to sonship, the redemption of our bodies. For in this hope we were saved. But hope that is seen is no hope at all. Who hopes for what they already have? But if we hope for what we do not yet have, we wait for it patiently.
>
> —*Romans 8:18–25*

Not only the disciples, not only the early church, not even only humanity but the *whole creation* groans to be united with the Creator. This is the nature of the world created by a Trinitarian

God, to be united with God, with its Source. We experience pain and suffering because we and those around us turn from God, again and again and again. We ignore the image of God in us when we choose ourselves over others, might over right, and security over trust in the One who made us.

Being the Image of God

> Then God said, "Let us make humankind in our image, according to our likeness; and let them have dominion over the fish of the sea, and over the birds of the air, and over the cattle, and over all the wild animals of the earth, and over every creeping thing that creeps upon the earth." So God created humankind in his image, in the image of God he created them; male and female he created them.
>
> —*Genesis 1:26–27 NRSV*

When I think about being made in the image of God, my first thought is of Adam and Eve, pre-sin. They care for the garden, which sustains them. They talk with God freely and without shame. They are at home in their embodied, fleshy selves. They live in a world without pain or sorrow. This ideal is hard to live up to, particularly for those of us who have never grown our own food or who are still unsure of how to approach God. Even harder for those of us brought up or self-conditioned to believe that our bodies are an earthly trap, to be wedged into submission or Spanx. Perhaps we're ashamed of our sexual desires or hate the parts that jiggle or can't move freely. The glorious firstborn of creation are an impossible ideal in a fallen world.

Adam and Eve aren't our only role models of the *imago Dei*. Paul refers twice to Jesus as the image of God, in the Colossians passage that opens this chapter and in 2 Corinthians 4:4: "The god of this age has blinded the minds of unbelievers, so that they cannot see the light of the gospel that displays the glory of Christ, who is the image of God." If we are dim images of the Creator, Christ is a perfect reflection, and we ought to take seriously his message of good news for all—rich and poor, powerless and powerful. The good news of Christ is as good for the rich as it is for the poor, as good for the powerful as it is for the powerless. It is good news to be released from the shackles of conformity to a corrupt culture; good news that our riches aren't in worldly goods but in something much longer lasting.

Being made in the image of God. What does it mean? Do we look like God? Are we Godlike? Because I have to tell you, I don't feel very much like God when I'm trying to convince my six-year-old to eat dinner in a timely fashion, or when I read about yet another Terrible Thing I Can't Control.

We humans have a troubling historical habit of insisting on identifying ourselves as "the climax, the most significant, of all of God's creative work"[9] without any examination of how that interpretation has damaged humanity's relationship with God, with one another, and with God's creation. In an exhaustive study of Genesis 1:26–28, biblical scholar J. Richard Middleton concludes that the most likely meaning of "image" and "likeness" is both representational and representative, and that these two attributes are intimately connected.[10] In other words, yes, humans are special, though human sin has certainly marred the image of God in us. But we also have a functional role in creation to represent God on earth.

When we get this representation wrong, we really get it wrong. Every violent abuse of power, every bullying act, is a mutilation of God's image and a violation of the stewardship with which we have been entrusted by the Creator who lovingly crafted and righteously cares for this world.

Middleton's charge to us is pointed. We ought to behave "as priests of creation, actively mediating divine blessing to the nonhuman world and—in a postfall situation—interceding on behalf of a groaning creation until that day when heaven and earth are redemptively transformed to fulfill God's purposes for justice and shalom."[11] To be made in the image of God is not a license to conquer and kill; it is a charge to keep and till. We are to protect the creation and actively work for its reconciliation back to God. It is a Trinitarian charge.

What Does It Mean to Be Made in the Image of a Trinitarian God?

> But because of his great love for us, God, who is rich in mercy, made us alive with Christ even when we were dead in transgressions—it is by grace you have been saved.
>
> —*Ephesians 2:4–5*

The Scriptures tell us to prepare for a new city. For some of us, that has meant fixing our eyes on a distant heaven and white-knuckling our few decades on earth in the hope that we'll get our own room beyond the pearly gates. But the fact of a Trinitarian God requires a different approach. Native American Christian and theologian Randy Woodley reminds us that "Christ is not just King, but Creator. Kings come and go, but the Creator is eternal. When we begin to realize the cosmic implications of Christ as Creator, temporal concepts like governments, king-doms, and rulers fade in comparison."[12] Woodley suggests that a helpful, transhistorical way to think about the kingdom of God is as the "Community of Creation."

It makes sense, after all. Jesus declared over and over again that the kingdom of heaven is *here*. Jesus, the incarnation of God on earth, brought the new city to us. We aren't climbing a stairway to heaven to reach it and escape this earthly hell in the process; we need only look around and act as if it is already here.

The prophet Jeremiah anticipates this radical move. As he looks at the ruins of the city of Jerusalem, God tells him, "I will bring health and healing to it. . . . I will cleanse them from all the sin they have committed against me and will forgive all their sins of rebellion against me. Then this city will bring me renown, joy, praise and honor before all nations on earth. . . . In this place, desolate and without people or animals—in all its towns there will again be pastures for shepherds to rest with their flocks" (Jer. 33:6, 8–9, 12).

The apostle Paul echoes the promise of the new creation in his second letter to the Corinthians. They are bemoaning the weight and torment of the earth, eager for Christ's return, not knowing that he will not come again in their lifetimes. To these patiently impatient followers of Jesus, Paul says:

> For Christ's love compels us, because we are convinced that one died for all, and therefore all died. And he died for all, that those who live should no longer live for themselves but for him who died for them and was raised again.
>
> So from now on we regard no one from a worldly point of view. Though we once regarded Christ in this way, we do so no longer. Therefore, if anyone is in Christ, the new creation has come: The old has gone, the new is here! All this is from God, who reconciled us to himself through Christ and gave us the ministry of reconciliation: that God was reconciling the world to himself in Christ, not counting people's sins against them. And he has committed to us the message of reconciliation. We are therefore Christ's ambassadors, as though God were making his appeal through us. We implore you on Christ's behalf: Be reconciled to God.
>
> —2 Corinthians 5:14–20

This is a radical new way to look at the world. Motivated and sustained by the love of Christ, we share the good news that all the old ways of living, being, and relating have been replaced by the reconciliation of all creation to the Creator. Our ministry—our calling—is reconciliation, returning and leading others to a life in Christ that is Trinitarian—communal, interdependent, and just—by its very nature.

This calling is a powerful and perhaps dangerous charge, particularly in our age, where we have elevated isolation, independence, and dominance to an idolatrous level. We don't have to look far to see that humans have learned to use power in shocking and devastating ways. We have failed, again and again, to remember that "the power of the triune God is not coercive, but creative, sacrificial, and empowering love; and the glory of the triune God consists not in dominating others but in sharing life with others."[13]

Further Questions

I can anticipate some questions that might have come to the surface as we've moved through this exploration of what it means to be made in the image of the Trinitarian God.

In this Trinitarian, perichoretic world, it sounds like everything is divine. Are you saying we should worship creation?

Absolutely not. We worship God, the Creator of all, but creation is not separate from the Creator. Just as Christ reconciles us back to God, so too he reconciles the whole creation.[14] It is both physically and spiritually dangerous to neglect to see the world as the work of God and under God's protection. Physically dangerous because when we neglect to act as interdependent beings in creation, we ruin it for ourselves and everyone else. Consider how many species of animal are now extinct because of human habitat encroachment, human-caused damage to local ecosystems, and human use of the ocean as a giant trash can.

Spiritually dangerous because the mentality that breeds a "might makes right" worldview has no end. Acknowledging these facts requires not worship but respect and care. Oppression begets oppression. The practice of turning away from God is perfected in the oppression of others.

What is the distinction between humans and animals? Isn't such a distinction important?

I ask, what is the motivation for identifying distinction? Is it to rationalize or justify a behavior? Is it to better understand our role in the world? To be a better follower of Jesus? How might one's actions based on a real or perceived distinction change depending on the answers to these questions?

Middleton points out that "most patristic, medieval, and modern interpreters typically asked not an exegetical, but a speculative question: In what way are humans *like* God and *unlike* animals?"[15] The answer was and still is typically rooted in the notion that humans are the only rational beings, the only beings capable of using language or tools, the only beings who respond to God, and so on—all false suppositions.

Murray Gow, a theologian from New Zealand, points out that talking about the events of Genesis 2 and 3 as "the fall" is inaccurate at best and potentially harmful to our reading of the text. The Hebrew word for "fall" isn't used in these chapters. Instead, what's described is an act of disobedience, of deviation from the covenant, a sin that "produces alienation between God and humans, between humans and their environment, between human and human, and even in the depths of their own being, the alienated self."[16] That description is instructive, isn't it? When we think about a fall, we think of coming down from a height and inevitably wonder how we can scramble back up. But if we consider instead that we have been operating for a few millennia out of covenant with God *and* with one another *and* with creation *and* with ourselves, perhaps what is distinct about us is that we are exceptionally unaware. Unaware of how our actions impact those around the world, unaware of how the stories we tell ourselves condition our behavior to such an extent that we can no longer tell fiction from reality, unaware of the most basic facts about how food gets from farm to table.

And yet.

Jesus was incarnated as a human man. He lived a human life and died a human death. What really sets us apart is that even though human hands have wreaked havoc and disharmony for centuries, God chose us—you and me—to bear his image and to be ambassadors of Christ's reconciling work to the whole world. We are representatives of God in creation, and though we have done a remarkably terrible job, God has kept covenant with us again and again and again.

Being "set apart" can be a blessing or a curse. The Israelites were set apart. God blessed Abraham so that he would be a blessing to others (Gen. 12:2). Psalm 4:3 tells us that the faithful are set apart. Paul was set apart for the gospel of God (Rom. 1:1) and was set apart to proclaim that gospel to Gentiles, a group that had been considered unclean. We are called to a radical unity in creation, slave with free, Jew with Greek, man with woman. We are called to be holy, to reflect the light that casts out all darkness. We are called over and over again to resist conforming to the habits of a broken covenant, to be set free (Gal. 5:1), to discern what is good and acceptable and perfect (Rom. 12:2).

The better question to ask is not "What is the distinction between humans and all other creation?" but "How can I use God's blessing to bless others?"

Are we really called to be in community with animals?

Yes. From the first days of creation, animals and humans were intimately connected. Genesis 2 tells us that Adam named the animals, an act that denotes intimacy and familiarity. We'll see in the coming chapters that God includes laws governing the treatment of animals in the instructions given to the Israelites. More important, though, animals are included in the images of restored creation throughout the Bible. God's covenant is with humans *and* animals (see, e.g., Gen. 9:9–17; Hos. 2:18). We are told that animals praise God (Pss. 148 and 150) and that every creature will praise God in heaven (Rev. 4:8–9; 5:13). It might seem sentimental to think of animals in heaven, like we are just looking for a reunion with a beloved childhood pet, but God created the whole world and the whole world points to the power and majesty of its Creator.

If God is so communal, why did he demand animal sacrifices and command the wholesale slaughter of some towns?

In the nineteenth century a Christian church in Philadelphia required members to be vegetarian and to abstain from alcohol. They were called Bible Christians, and they prided themselves on a literal interpretation of Scripture. No surprise that they also wrestled with the depiction of animal sacrifice in the Old Testament. Their pastor decreed that it was improbable that the Israelites had sacrificed living animals and came instead to the far-out conclusion that the Israelites had used wafers impressed with the likeness of goats, bulls, doves, and so on. In other words, when we want to believe something, we are capable of some pretty impressive(ly illogical) mental gymnastics.

While I appreciate a good deal about the Bible Christians, I think in this particular interpretation of Scripture, they were pretty far off the mark. Nothing challenges my belief in the veracity of Scripture more than reading the Old Testament slaughter requirements or an account of a village and all of its inhabitants being burned to the ground. God's instruction to Moses to tell the priest to tear the head off a bird and rip her open by her wings is difficult reading for a gal who has seen modern-day slaughterhouse workers do the same (a sacrifice to American gluttony, in that case, and not to God).

I don't have an easy answer for this.

After introducing God as the Source of all, and Jesus as not a lesser being but as God's own self, John reminds us that "in him was life, and that life was the light of all mankind. The light shines in the darkness, and the darkness has not overcome it. . . . The Word became flesh and made his dwelling among us. We have seen his glory, the glory of the one and only Son, who came from the Father, full of grace and truth" (John 1:4–5, 14). Christ is the loving Creator. Christ is the genesis of all, the sustainer of all, and the hope of all. The lion of the tribe of Judah became a slaughtered lamb, the ultimate and final sacrifice, ushering in the kingdom of God.

I could say that these passages represent a different time, that Christ's sacrifice changed everything, and that's true, but that doesn't address our Trinitarian problem. How can God—whose nature is to be in relationship and who desires that the work of his hands be restored—insist that humans kill animals as a condition of their approach, when the act of killing is the ultimate severance of relationship between victim and killer, between killer and the killer's self (for surely every time we take a life, we turn further inward)?

Rich Stearns, president of the international relief organization World Vision, wrote a moving article for *Christianity Today* about sacrifice. How it must have looked and smelled. A visceral, horrific reminder of the bloody, ugly reality of life separate from God, a separation brought on by human rejection of the world God had carefully pieced together from his own breath, formed with his own fingers.[17] A separation that brought death to earthly relationships and communities, and thus to our bodies and to animal bodies. With responsibility comes culpability. I imagine that God felt every slit of the blade, every drop of blood that fell, every broken neck and bruised body. I imagine that he wept at every lost life. I imagine that when Jesus wept and prayed at Gethsemane, and that when he was hanging on the cross, he also felt every drop of blood, broken bone, and bruised body that had suffered before him and that has suffered since. The embodiment of separation from God is death. Jesus' sacrifice restored the break, bridged the deep divide that sin created, so that we no longer need to feel blood on our hands, we no longer need to break a neck, we no longer need to be the cause of fear and suffering in order to approach God.

What Comes Next?

After declaring that we humans are made in the image of God, the Creator gives us dominion over the earth. We are charged to till and keep the creation on God's behalf. In the next chapter, we will build on our understanding of the *imago Dei* to explore our corresponding responsibility.

Discussion Questions

1. What words do you associate with the idea of being made in God's image?
2. What rights and responsibilities come with the human designation as being made in the *imago Dei*?
3. How does the discussion of the Trinitarian nature of God affect your understanding of what it means to be made in the image of God?
4. In what practical ways can you demonstrate the image of God in your daily life?

CHAPTER 2

Dominion and Stewardship

A Charge to Keep We Have

And the twenty-four elders, who were seated on their thrones before God, fell on their faces and worshiped God, saying: "We give thanks to you, Lord God Almighty, the One who is and who was, because you have taken your great power and have begun to reign. The nations were angry, and your wrath has come. The time has come for judging the dead, and for rewarding your servants the prophets and your people who revere your name, both great and small— and for destroying those who destroy the earth."

—*Revelation 11:16–18*

We read in Genesis that God tells humans to care for the created world, to have dominion, to fill and subdue, to till and keep. Elsewhere in the Old Testament, God gives the Israelites specific instructions on stewarding creation well, and the prophets rail against political and economic systems that remove God's people from the intimate and important task of bringing forth food from the land and sharing in God's creative abundance. Amos, for instance, decries the early agribusiness, the commodification of staple crops, which forced families to purchase life-giving grain instead of growing it themselves (Amos 8:4–6).[1] We listen to the teachings of Jesus knowing that he was raised from infancy in the centuries-old agrarian traditions of the Jewish people. And Revelation warns that those who would destroy God's creation will themselves be destroyed.

I don't have a green thumb. Or really any green appendages. I've never planted and harvested my own food. I have trouble keeping the hardiest of houseplants alive. Not long ago, most of us in the United States were active participants in some aspect of growing our own food. We had vegetable gardens and fruit trees, we grew our own wheat to make bread, hens in our back yards provided eggs, and milk from a family cow would be used to make butter and cheese. Today, less than 1 percent of the US population cite farming as their primary occupation. Fewer than 2 percent of us live on farms. And 8.5 percent of farms provide a whopping 63 percent of agricultural sales (meaning that a small number of farms produce the majority of what we eat).[2]

Instead of being people who cultivate and produce, we are people who consume. Biblical scholar Ellen Davis aptly diagnoses the phenomenon: "In an earlier age, 'consumption' denoted a disease that wasted the body; the same term now names the sickness that lays waste to the earth."[3] Here are just a few of the signs and wonders of a world gripped by consumption:

- Dr. Fred Davies, senior science advisor for the Bureau for Food Security of the US Agency for International Development: "For the first time in human history, food production will be limited on a global scale by the availability of land, water and energy. . . . Food issues could become as politically destabilizing by 2050 as energy issues are today."[4]
- António Guterres, UN High Commissioner for Refugees: "In 2008, 36 million people were displaced by natural disasters. At least 20 million of those people were driven from their homes by disasters . . . like drought and rising sea level."[5]

- "In 2013, about 1.3 billion people lived in water-scarce regions."[6]
- "The intensity, frequency, and duration of North Atlantic hurricanes, as well as the frequency of the strongest hurricanes, have all increased since the early 1980s."[7]
- World Food Programme: "In some countries, yields from rain-fed agriculture could fall by 50 percent by 2020."[8]
- The last decade has seen the extinction of the Eastern cougar, the Western black rhinoceros, the Pinta Island tortoise, the baiji dolphin, and others.[9]
- "In the last 500 years, human activity is known to have forced 869 species to extinction (or extinction in the wild). . . . The current species extinction rate is estimated to be between 1,000 and 10,000 times higher than the natural or 'background' rate."[10]
- "Every day, 2 million tons of sewage and other [wastes] drain into the world's waters. Every year, more people die from unsafe water than from all forms of violence, including war."[11]
- Environmental Protection Agency: "Approximately 75 million people nationwide lived in counties with pollution levels above the primary NAAQS [National Ambient Air Quality Standards] in 2013."[12]
- Center for Biological Diversity: "Of the more than 300,000 known species of plants, the IUCN [International Union for Conservation of Nature] has evaluated only 12,914 species, finding that about 68 percent of evaluated plant species are threatened with extinction."[13]
- Researchers found "'reliable declines' in the amount of protein, calcium, phosphorus, iron, riboflavin (vitamin B2) and vitamin C" in 43 different fruits and vegetables between 1950 and 1999. Another "analysis of nutrient data from 1975 to 1997 found that average calcium levels

in 12 fresh vegetables dropped 27 percent; iron levels 37 percent; vitamin A levels 21 percent; and vitamin C levels 30 percent."[14] In other words, the food we eat is losing nutritional value. An apple today is no longer as nourishing as an apple eaten by your parents or grandparents was.

- Most modern US farmers are ensnared in a corrupt political and economic system that leaves them barely enough to survive.[15]

In summary: the planet is becoming less habitable and less sustaining not only for humans but also for animal and plant species.

It is popular in some circles to blame Christianity for the global climate crisis. In an arrogant and power-hungry grab for dominion and comfort, Christians have led the charge to trample and conquer green spaces, suck "natural resources" from the earth with no thought for the long-term consequences, and create systems of mass breeding and mass killing of animals to feed an insatiable appetite for flesh. So goes the old tune.

But Christians needn't be quick to start whistling along.

Our tradition is not one of consumption but rather one of cultivation. Our tradition is not the acquisition of power but the sharing of it. Our tradition calls us not to pillage the earth but to keep it.

New Testament scholar Richard Bauckham lays the blame for the current ecological crisis squarely at the feet of modernity. The ideals of materialism, consumerism, industrialization, commodification, and individualism "can be understood only as the supersession of Christian ideals, values and practice by post-Christian and secular modes of thought, goals and forms of life."[16]

That's not to say that Christians haven't been complicit in the crisis. Secular modernity is now so embedded in the church that many in my generation know nothing *but* church shopping, pastor as CEO, therapy instead of theology, and individualism over community. Some of us have been misled our entire lives; others have lost track of who we are and why we are here. Rather than listening to God's Word and learning from the biblical texts, we have swallowed modern lies about what it means to be made in God's image and how we are to live that out. I am as guilty as anyone else in my failure to live into our calling to govern well.

In this chapter we will talk about what it means to have dominion, to fill and subdue, to till and keep. We'll discuss the biblical view of humans' role in creation and how Christ followers especially are called to care for the world in which we live.

What Does Dominion Mean?

> You cause the grass to grow for the cattle, and plants for people to use, to bring forth food from the earth, and wine to gladden the human heart, oil to make the face shine, and bread to strengthen the human heart. The trees of the LORD are watered abundantly. . . . May the glory of the LORD endure forever; may the LORD rejoice in his works—who looks on the earth and it trembles, who touches the mountains and they smoke.
>
> —*Psalm 104:14–16, 31–32 NRSV*

Though my young son would prefer to read Lego character encyclopedias, occasionally I am able to find a long story that captures his attention and imagination. The other night we finished reading *The Magician's Nephew* by C. S. Lewis. It had been more than a quarter century since I read the book in its entirety. I had forgotten that at its heart is a creation narrative, a story of the beginning of Narnia, a retelling of the Genesis creation story. The lion Aslan (God) calls the new world into being out of nothing. Grasses and trees and birds and living creatures of all sorts rise from the ground in response to the lion's song. Lewis paints a vivid portrait of God's creative activity.

But it is Lewis's treatment of the animals and the assignment of human dominion in creation that took my breath away. "Creatures, I give you yourselves," says the Creator to the chosen animals. "I give to you forever this land of Narnia. I give you the woods, the fruits, the rivers. I give you the stars and I give you myself. The Dumb Beasts whom I have not chosen are yours also. Treat them gently and cherish them. . . ."[17] Animals don't *belong* to humans here; they belong to themselves. And those creatures to whom Aslan has entrusted the care of other creatures are accountable not to humans, but to the Creator. They communicate with Aslan without human mediation, and they worship and serve him of their own accord.

Shortly thereafter, to a surprised and humble London cabby and his wife, the Creator bestows the titles of King and Queen of Narnia. Feeling unworthy, the cabby tries to beg off, claiming he is unqualified for the post. In response Aslan asks:

- "Can you use a spade and a plow and raise food out of the earth?"
- "Can you rule these creatures kindly and fairly, remembering that they are not slaves like the dumb beasts of the world you were born in, but Talking Beasts and free subjects?"
- "Would you bring up your children and grandchildren to do the same?"
- "You wouldn't have favorites either among your own children or among other creatures or let any hold another under or use it hardly?"
- "And if enemies came against the land . . . and there was war, would you be the first in charge and the last in retreat?"[18]

Note the questions here are not "Are you stronger than the animals?" or "Can you control the wild beasts?" or even "Do you have good use for them?" The questions highlight the humans' ability to cultivate and care for and exercise concern, restraint, and protection.

Lewis's interpretation of the Genesis creation account and the blessing of dominion is not far from that of biblical scholars.

And yes, dominion is a blessing, not a divine right. "Blessing, as the biblical writers conceive it, is a kind of ecological phenomenon; it connects God and the creatures in a complex of interlocking relationships."[19] When God blessed Abraham, it was so that "you will be a blessing. . . . All peoples on earth will be blessed through you" (Gen. 12:2–3). Like the first humans, Abraham was charged with sharing God's care, not hoarding it. And when the nation of Israel failed to heed this charge, curses followed, much as Lewis's Empress Jadis was cursed when she ate the silver apple, for "that is what happens to those who pluck and eat fruits at the wrong time and in the wrong way. The fruit is good, but they loathe it ever after."[20]

The witch in *The Magician's Nephew* desired power above all else, the conquest of the world. That's not the kind of dominion that the biblical writers envisioned.

Translation and interpretation of the Hebrew language in the Old Testament are not as straightforward as some of us type A personalities would like. Each word can have multiple meanings, depending on the context in which it was written and in which it appears in the text. Here's Genesis 1:28: "God blessed them and said to them, 'Be fruitful and increase in number; fill the earth and subdue it. Rule over the fish in the sea and the birds in the sky and over every living creature that moves on the ground.'" God then goes on to prescribe a vegan diet for humans and animals, which is significant, but we'll come back to that later.

The three words in Genesis 1:28 on which much of our view

of our place in creation is based are *subdue*, *rule* (or *dominion*), and *over*. Some scholars claim that the words for "subdue" and "dominion" indicate that "creation is clearly subservient to those whom God has blessed, but there is no suggestion that they should feel free to abuse and mistreat creation, which would be clearly inappropriate in light of their creation in the image of God."[21] If you think the way I used to, this is a comfortable interpretation and one that might not require us to change much about what we do or how we live. As long as we mean well and aren't too selfish, we can justify pursuing our desires and assuage any nagging sense of dis-ease.

But there are alternatives to this comfortable interpretation that deserve careful, prayerful consideration.

The Hebrew word commonly translated as "rule" or "domin-ion" in Genesis 1:28 is *r-d-h*; however, Davis translates *r-d-h* and its preposition as "mastery among" rather than "dominion over" and cites other uses of the word in Scripture that describe a shepherd traveling with the flock.[22] I cringe at the word "mas-ter," which to me has deeply embedded associations with the man-made institution of slavery. But that modern, broken relationship doesn't exist in the text. Let's widen our view from the one phrase "dominion over" or "mastery among" and read the verse in light of the whole creation story, then in light of the whole scriptural arc. Genesis 1:26 reminds us that our mastery among creation is conditional on our creation in the image of God. Davis's translation reads: "Let us make humankind as our image, after our likeness, *that they may* exercise mastery among the fish of the sea."[23] And, as we discovered in the last chapter, to be made in the image of God is to pursue a life of righteousness, mutual submission, and generative love. Perhaps that is why the cultivation and care of plant life (plant life, which God intends as the sole source of food for all humans and animals) is the prominent command of the following verses.[24]

Job is a book about faith in the midst of suffering. Have you ever noticed how much of the book references the human relationship with the rest of creation? Or God's power in creation, in contrast with human dependence on God? The whole of God's answer to Job in chapters 38 through 41 is a declaration of God's might, God's provision, God's dominion. The human place in this dominion is to humbly ask God for guidance, discipline, and the will to obey.

Like Davis, Bauckham finds that humanity's status in creation is a dominion within, not above.[25] As God reminds us in Job, only God is transcendent. Human mastery or dominion among other creatures is a highly qualified affair, with limitations (e.g., eat only plants), and is driven by a sense of the familial.[26] When Israel demanded a king, God set similar limitations: the king was to be one of the community, to obey God diligently, and to refrain from "exalting himself above other members of the community" (Deut. 17:20 NRSV).

Just as the cabby was allowed to rule Narnia only under the premise of care and cultivation, human beings were assigned the task of feeding themselves with plants and working the earth to help ensure God's provision for all creatures.

The role of humanity in creation is a Trinitarian one. In his extensive study of the historical interpretation of dominion, Bauckham finds a Trinitarian vision in which "the hierarchy is virtually subverted by mutuality: the obedience which the creatures owe to humanity is reciprocated by an obedience of humanity to the creatures . . . a kind of mutual and humble deference in the common service of the creatures to their Creator."[27] In other words, since all of creation exists to serve and glorify the Creator, "do unto others" applies in the context of *all human* relationships: human to human, human to animal, human to tree, and human to air.

What Does It Mean to Fill and Subdue? Till and Keep?

> Follow my decrees and be careful to obey my laws, and you will live safely in the land. Then the land will yield its fruit, and you will eat your fill and live there in safety. . . .
>
> The land must not be sold permanently, because the land is mine and you reside in my land as foreigners and strangers. Throughout the land that you hold as a possession, you must provide for the redemption of the land.
>
> —*Leviticus 25:18–19, 23–24*

God commanded humankind to fill the earth and subdue it, according to Genesis 1. In Genesis 2, God places the human creature in the garden of Eden "to work it and take care of it" (Gen. 2:15; the NRSV says "to till it and keep it"). The kind of fill and subdue and till and keep practiced by many today is counter to the symbiotic harmony that flowed from God's creative spree. Modern industrial influences tell us that to subdue means to conquer violently and that to keep is to claim ownership. But reading these verses, and the whole of the Old Testament, through the eyes of those who wrote them, through the eyes of people who were intimately and daily connected with the land, even during exile, requires a different interpretation.

It's critical to note that the Hebrews were reminded again and again that the land was not theirs but God's. God created the land to provide sustenance for all creation, through the form of plants, and the living was easy until the human creatures staged a power grab and ate from the one tree that was forbidden to them. A lot of us today think that technology holds the answers to our problems—that human-driven engineering will alleviate human-created catastrophes. The first human couple, Adam and Eve, were the first creatures to learn the hard lesson that the pursuit of knowledge over obedience to God's commands has disastrous consequences. The first sin brought disharmony between humans and the whole of creation. No longer were humans and animals at peace together. Rather than abundant, divine provision, food was to be scratched from the cursed ground through toil and sweat. Soon, humans began killing one another.

Humans are not the only creatures told to fill the earth in Genesis 1. The same command is given to the birds and fish (Gen. 1:22). God calls the earth to put forth plants (Gen. 1:11), and when the earth responds in obedience, God calls it good. Davis points out that the human activity that drastically depletes habitats and contributes to the extinction of countless plant and animal species makes a mockery of the command to "fill."[28] Instead of ensuring abundant room for creation (including humans) to flourish, we are paving paradise. Instead of trusting God to provide, allowing our faith to move mountains, we're using dynamite, reducing mountains to piles of toxic rubble in order to access coal. Instead of "Till, baby, till," it's "Drill, baby, drill," as we shoot poison into the ground to release natural gas. When tap water starts to burn, surely we must wonder if the end is at hand.

Bauckham posits, "To subdue the earth is to take possession and to work the soil in order to make it yield more food for humans than it would otherwise do. . . . Humans are not to fill the earth and subdue it to the extent of leaving no room and no sustenance for the other creatures who share the earth with them. God has given them too the right to live from the soil."[29] The sentiment seems right, but let's look at the clues we might find through other uses of the word *subdue* (*kabash*).[30]

Kabash is used in the books of Numbers (32:22, 29) and Joshua (18:1) in reference to subduing or subjecting land in the midst of war. In 2 Samuel 8:11, the word is used to describe nations defeated by King David. The meaning may shift a bit in 1 Chronicles 22:18 as David describes a sort of harmony: "Is not the LORD your God with you? And has he not granted you rest on every side? . . . The land is subject to the LORD and to his people." In 2 Chronicles 28:10, the prophet Oded uses *kabash* in his condemnation of the Israelites' intent to enslave their kin, members of the tribe of Judah. Nehemiah 5 tells us that when labor and money were poured into the rebuilding of the walls of Jerusalem, at the expense of cultivating the land, many people fell into hunger and poverty, forcing their children into slavery and losing the vineyards and fields for which they had been charged to care. In Esther 7:8, *kabash* is commonly translated as "assault" but may mean that Haman was flinging himself at Esther's feet, pleading for mercy. Jeremiah 34 describes God's anger at Israel's violation of the community covenant, requiring the nation to release any kin held as servants or slaves during the Sabbath year. Here, *kabash* refers to the subjugation of brother to brother, sister to sister. Micah 7:19 tells us that God will "tread our sins underfoot," a prophecy echoed in Zechariah 9:15. I have argued elsewhere that the prophet's reclamation of the word in these latter passages calls modern readers to consider that perhaps we ought to subdue not the earth itself, but that which threatens to undermine the *shalom* of God's symbiotic creation.[31]

Davis suggests that the use of a word commonly understood for its violent undertones was the writer's intention. Spoken to a people for whom forceful expulsion, slavery, exile, and war were tangible experiences, the word jars the hearer, forces them to pay attention.[32] Rather than a statement of reality, that humans have successfully cultivated and cared for the land in such a way as to allow abundant flourishing of life with substantive provision for all of God's creation, Davis argues that the Genesis writer is sending a pointed reminder to a people who have repeatedly *failed* this most basic charter. "Thus the larger story of the beginnings of humanity and the world, traced through the first three chapters of the Bible, shows the essential connection between accurate seeing and action appropriate to our place, and it suggests that the privileged status of humans among the creatures is a divine intention still awaiting realization."[33]

Just as we must view human dominion in the light of our being created in the image of God, so must we view the charge to subdue and keep the earth in the light of God's intent for creation: to protect *all* of God's created life; to cultivate plants to feed *every* living being; and to tend our earthen home in such a way as to ensure the flourishing of life and the freedom of every being to praise its Creator.

Does Jesus Have Anything to Say about Stewardship?

> Therefore let us stop passing judgment on one another. Instead, make up your mind not to put any stumbling block or obstacle in the way of a brother or sister. I am convinced, being fully persuaded in the Lord Jesus, that nothing is unclean in itself. But if anyone regards something as unclean, then for that person it is unclean. If your brother or sister is distressed because of what you eat, you are no longer acting in love. Do not by your eating destroy someone for whom Christ died. Therefore do not let what you know is good be spoken of as evil. For the kingdom of God is not a matter of eating and drinking, but of righteousness, peace and joy in the Holy Spirit.
>
> —*Romans 14:13–17*

Unlike the Hebrew Scriptures, Jesus' teachings aren't replete with instructions for caring for the land or creation. Of course, he uses imagery that farmers and shepherds would understand, being rooted in the land and attuned to its rhythms. Yet we shouldn't take this perceived silence from Jesus on creation care as a license to ride roughshod over land, water, air, and animals, because Jesus isn't speaking from a blank slate. The traditions and teachings of the Old Testament were ingrained in him from childhood. So while Jesus may not have said anything specifically about animal protection, "[Jesus] places himself clearly within the Jewish ethical and legal tradition that held that God requires his people to treat their fellow-creatures, the animals, with compassion and consideration."[34]

In the next chapter, we'll look at what Jesus *did* teach and think about what that means for us today.

Further Questions

I have tried in this chapter to draw a broad vision of human dominion and stewardship of creation. Here are a few more specific questions (and answers) that frequently come up in conversations about this topic:

Aren't humans the mediators between God and creation?

Simply put? No. Bauckham argues forcefully: "Of this arrogant assertion that only through human mediation can the rest of creation be itself in relation to God there is not a trace in the Scriptures."[35] Humans were put into a complete world, a world ready for habitation, a world in which creation worshiped the Creator quite apart from human intervention, a perfect world, not requiring radical reshaping (and, in fact, one that is arguably suffering under global industrialization).[36] The first human was given specific limits of power: eat only plants; don't eat fruit from that tree. Adam's dominion was not totalitarian, was not complete. The prophets Jeremiah and Isaiah both highlight the devastation that results from trying to operate outside of those limits (Isaiah 24; Jeremiah 4).[37]

"In the beginning was the Word, and the Word was with God, and the Word was God. . . . Through him all things were made; without him nothing was made that has been made" (John 1:1, 3). Jesus, and only Jesus, is the mediator of creation.[38] "In his creative love God is united with creation, which is his Other, giving it space, time and liberty in his own infinite life."[39] God desires the reconciliation of all bodies back to their Creator, and this happens not through humans, but through Jesus.

As stewards, don't we have freedom to choose what we want to do with the creation? We're its keepers.

The Creator God has given all creation freedom. Freedom to choose to love God and love our neighbor; freedom to pursue justice, righteousness, and peace; and freedom to reject God, turn away from our Creator, and seek our own gain. Freedom to choose how we use our freedom. Moltmann points out that "the more power mankind acquires over nature, the more dangerous the human history of freedom becomes, and the more urgent the orientation towards the realm of the Good. Otherwise people could not acquire power over the power they have, and could make no use of their liberty."[40]

When God created humans, our responsibility in creation was to maintain the thriving and abundant food system that God created to feed the whole world (plants).[41] The abuse of our freedom leads not only to our own detriment, but also to the extinction of both plant and animal life. Furthermore, our industrialized food system not only breeds and kills billions of animals each year (twenty-seven billion in the United States alone) but also pollutes the ground, air, and water; robs the soil of nutrients; fosters chronic and deadly diseases; and causes the humans who work within the system both physical and psychological harm. If this is "freedom," then the "captivity" of dependence is preferable.

Don't we need to eat meat?

Most of us do not need to eat meat, and certainly not in the quantities to which modern humans have become accustomed. Before I went vegan many years ago, I ate meat a minimum of three times a day. Even my salads were covered in meat (and cheese and eggs and dairy-based dressings). After I adopted a vegan diet, months passed before I stopped craving meat. A strong and growing number of vegan ultra-athletes are proving that peak physical performance is possible on plant-based diets. Just look at Jim Morris (vegan bodybuilder), Brendan Brazier (champion triathlete), Carl Lewis (Olympic medal–winning runner), Catra Corbett (ultra-marathoner), and other jaw-droppingly fit vegan athletes making headlines today.

Most of us don't *need* to eat meat; we want to. We like the taste. We have strong positive associations of meat-eating at family events and holidays. We may think it's convenient.

Some argue that God meant for us to eat meat or it wouldn't taste so good. But many things that taste or feel delightful aren't good for us and don't do anything to bring us closer to God. In fact, these very things can work to push us farther out of God's will and deeper into our own.

Davis says, "Appreciation and enjoyment of the creatures are the hallmark of God's dominion and therefore the standard by which our own attempts to exercise dominion must be judged."[42] Some cynical people might retort with the classic, "I love all God's creatures . . . right next to the mashed potatoes." They are perhaps avoiding a critical look at long-standing personal habits and centuries-old traditions and refusing to ask whether they are pleasing to God.

Can't we use animals as we wish as long as we treat them well?

This question is sometimes framed as a debate between "animal rights" and "animal welfare." People who promote animal welfare believe it's moral to use animals provided that they are not egregiously pained during the process. People who promote animal rights argue that animals are not ours to use. Secular proponents of animal rights posit that animals ought to be left alone because they belong to themselves. I argue that animals ought to be cared for because they are God's. I think we are called to generosity beyond the letter of the law, beyond what is easy or within one's means. This is God's posture with us and part of our call as the church: generosity beyond measure.

Then there is the matter of practicality. At one time, when there were fewer people on the planet and they ate mostly plants, perhaps it was possible for a sheep or a cow to be born, to be raised in a way that honored her sheep-ness or cow-ness, and to be killed quickly, with a minimum of pain or fear or impact on her fellow flock or herd. Perhaps. But if it ever truly existed, that time is long gone. The idea that it is "bad business" to abuse a cow who is raised for flesh or milk no longer applies in our context.[43]

When I was in high school, our biology class did a chicken-hatching/imprinting experiment. I fell in love with my little chick, Simon, who was injured in an avoidable accident and spent nights as he recovered curled next to my mother's collarbone or nestled in my hair. Wary of the fate that awaited him if I returned him to my biology teacher at the end of the experiment, I insisted on keeping him, but it was a different time and urban homesteading hadn't yet made its comeback. My dad found a family in our church who ran a small farm just outside of town who had room for Simon. I tearfully handed his fluffy yellow body over on Saturday morning and watched as he settled in next to an orphaned newborn duck the family was also caring for. Simon had a good life. He ran around; he was his chicken self. Then another rooster came along and my dad let me know one evening that the family had killed and eaten Simon.

I was sad, but not too sad. It seemed practical. A good life, probably not a terrible end. Certainly nothing like dying on an industrial slaughter line. I was still eating chickens then, so anger would have been hypocritical, and I knew that.

But now? Now I think that was a wasted death. An unnecessary death. A death too soon. Because no matter how lovely an animal's life is, we don't need to kill them to survive or thrive. It's wrong to take life unnecessarily. Jesus was so opposed to violence and killing that he ordered Peter to put his sword away when Roman soldiers came to arrest Jesus and the eager apostle cut off the ear of the high priest's servant.

Meat comes only from killing God's animals. Can we find a better way?

Discussion Questions

1. What do you think is our role as humans, and as Christians, in the created world?
2. How have you interpreted dominion in the past? How has your reading of this chapter influenced your view?
3. Do you think eating meat is a sin? What about other uses of animals?
4. Is there a conflict between being a steward and profiting from the use of land or animals?

CHAPTER 3

Loving the Other

The Greatest of These

> But to you who are listening I say: Love your enemies, do good to those who hate you, bless those who curse you, pray for those who mistreat you.
>
> —*Luke 6:27–28*

I have never got along all that well with children. As a child, I chose books over other kids more often than not. I never had a huge group of friends, always preferring the steady company of a few intimates. As a high schooler, I got jobs in food service instead of spending my evenings and weekends babysitting for car insurance and spending money. So when I was pregnant with my son, I was grateful to read that some mothers don't instantly bond with their newborns and that it might take a while for him to grow on me, even after he'd grown in me.

Imagine my surprise, then, when at his birth I felt a visceral, overwhelming, aching love for this little purple-red creature. A love that has only increased as the years have gone by. A love that is courage-giving and terrifying, powerful and vulnerable and utterly confounding. Confounding in part because he's not always very nice to me. There is a lot of whining. A lot of ingratitude. Some screaming and tantrum throwing and "I hate yous." He can be demanding, spoiled, selfish . . . just really obnoxious. There are times when I want to roll my eyes, tell him to shut up, run away, show him how much worse he could have it.

But I love him with my whole heart. And when the day is over and he's *finally* asleep, I look at his face that is a mirror of my own, and I listen to him breathe, and I curl his no-longer-tiny fingers around mine and thank God for entrusting me with this miracle of life, this funny, sweet, smart, caring, imaginative, fast-growing boy.

As my son was born of me, we are born of God. The loving gaze with which I watch my son is tepid, the aching love I feel a shadow compared to the fire of love God carries for us.

And so it should come as no surprise that the God whose love catalyzed a universe asks us to love not only those who are easy to love, and not only those to whom we are biologically preconditioned to love, but those who are least like us and who like us least.

Grace is costly, and love is hard.

Jesus' life was an ode to love of and outreach to the "other." He gathered rejects; bridged social, religious, and economic divides; and turned the notions of hospitality, faithfulness, and justice on their heads. Piety is out; compassion is in. When Jesus tells the story of the good Samaritan, we learn that neighbors are those who love "the least of these." In this chapter, we will explore the limits of love. How are we called to extend mercy to "the least of these"? Who is our neighbor? And we will ask especially what it might mean to view animals as our creaturely neighbors and to extend neighborly love to them.

The Problem of Exclusion

Show me your faith without deeds, and I will show you my faith by my deeds. You believe that there is one God. Good! Even the demons believe that—and shudder.

. . . You see that a person is considered righteous by what they do and not by faith alone.

> In the same way, was not even Rahab the prostitute con-
> sidered righteous for what she did when she gave lodging to
> the spies and sent them off in a different direction? As the
> body without the spirit is dead, so faith without deeds is dead.
> —James 2:18–19, 24–26

Rahab wasn't the obvious choice to play the hero in the story of how the Israelites conquered Jericho. A Canaanite woman, understood to be either a prostitute or an innkeeper, she was independent, savvy, and probably single. None of these were particularly sought-after qualities in ancient Palestinian women. But she was open to the leading of the Holy Spirit and, because of her faithfulness, is listed as one of Jesus' ancestors in the gospel of Matthew.[1]

Throughout the Bible, God chooses surprising ways to share the story of God's love and fidelity to all creation. Saul was a murderous prosecutor before he became Paul the prolific teacher. Esther was a Jewish orphan girl before she saved her people from death. Jonah rebelled and made friends with a fish before returning to God as an obedient (but still obstinate) missionary. A donkey helped God drive home to Balaam the importance of listening for and responding to God. Jesus compares God's love of Jerusalem to the love of a mother hen for her chicks.

But despite this rich scriptural history of embrace, we continue to find creative and cruel ways to push others away from us, both physically (you stay in your part of town, I'll stay in mine) and spiritually (well, *I'd* never . . .). "We exclude because we want to be at the center and be there alone," says Croatian Christian and Yale University Divinity School professor of theology Miroslav Volf.[2] It's a tale as old as the prophets, who saw the Israelites abandon the Law in favor of adopting customs that allowed for the appropriation and consolidation of massive swaths of land. The Law was written in a way that ensured all would have "access to the productive resources (land, money, knowledge) so that they [had] the opportunity to earn a generous sufficiency of material necessities and be dignified participating members of the community."[3] This was Old Testament justice as it was intended. Because of sin, a few hoarded crops while the rest went hungry.

Exclusion starts off small, but the slope is slippery and steep. We annex a property here, a vineyard there. Choose to invite the nice new couple with the same skin color to join our small group instead of the couple with one or two members who are of a different hue. Tell ourselves pornography and sex trafficking are two different problems, it's just a taste, or just this once. Maybe everyone else is doing it, it's what we've always done, or we don't want to cause a scene.

Here's what happens as a result: "Perpetrators tirelessly generate their own innocence, and do so by the double strategy of denying the wrongdoing and re-interpreting the moral significance of their actions. This double strategy is fertile ground for ideologies by which systems and nations seek to mask a violence and oppression they perpetrate."[4] We become so conditioned to exclude that we are able both to deny we are doing anything wrong and to trick ourselves into thinking we're actually in the right and our actions are morally justified. This is how we justify abuse in many forms. This is how we tolerate structures of systemic evil that, to an outsider, would appear to be an outright rejection of the command to "do unto others."

Exclusion is not just slaughter or violent rejection, and this is part of what makes it such a dangerous practice. Volf points out that exclusion can take three additional forms: assimilation, domination, and abandonment.[5] I'll show how animals are affected by each form.

Exclusion by assimilation demands the subject of exclusion to give up their identity, to be subsumed into the identity of the dominant power. The animals we keep as pets, in zoos, and in circuses fall into this category. I keep my cats inside, because they will live longer and healthier lives as a result, but it's a life entirely unnatural to them. Zoos and circuses (are supposed to) provide food, shelter, and water to animals in their care, and they do, but the animals are forced to live decades in an existence far removed from the one God conceived for them on the sixth day, often separated from their families and without access to anything like the room to roam God provided or the ability to express the natural behaviors with which God imbued them. Have you seen a polar bear at a zoo in the United States in the summer? Or an elephant pacing alone? Being alive isn't always a life.

When we exclude by domination, we establish ourselves as superior beings. We exploit another for our own gain. This broad category describes *all* of our uses of animals when we are set to profit in some way. We justify our use of animals for food because they are "less than" us.

And when we exclude by abandonment, we simply ignore problems from which we benefit. It's safe to say that we've abandoned the care of wildlife, as our own sprawl and development have encroached on countless habitats around the globe. And when animal residents dare return to forage for food, make a nest, or seek shelter in a place where a tall tree once stood, they are trapped, poisoned, shot, shooed away, or run over.

The End of Exclusion

"Which of these three do you think was a neighbor to the man who fell into the hands of robbers?"

The expert in the law replied, "The one who had mercy on him."

Jesus told him, "Go and do likewise."

—*Luke 10:36–37*

Do you notice in the parable of the good Samaritan that the lawyer can't bring himself to say, "The Samaritan is the neighbor"? He instead refers to the merciful man as "the one." That one. The one over there who is not like me. How we want to distance ourselves from the other! Today, cranky from delaying lunch for too long and driving from my office to my home, I found myself thinking, "I'm the only decent driver in my neighborhood." I really meant it at the time!

In many ways we have conditioned ourselves to mark our special territory in the world, to show ourselves and others that we are set apart, different, special, better. And it's not a long leap from unleashing my cranky, unfocused outburst to giving a neighbor the cold shoulder to forming a lynch mob. Given time, separation by degrees is as divisive as separation by yards.

Jesus' lawyer friend had a hard time acknowledging the goodness of the Samaritan because he had been conditioned by his society to see Samaritans as other, as less-than. Motivated by the same inclusive love that catalyzed Jesus' followers to cross cultures in order to befriend and bring the good news to Gentile and Jew alike, Jesus makes the Samaritan underdog the hero of his tale.

On the heels of the devastating war in former Yugoslavia, Volf published *Exclusion and Embrace* to explore what it means to be a Christian and to reconcile with the other. In it Volf writes that "God's reception of hostile humanity into divine communion is a model for how human beings should relate to the other."[6]

Some Christians have rejected the notion of "animal rights" because secular advocates have argued for increases in animal protection and liberty on the premise that there are no meaningful differences between humans and animals. We now know that animals and humans alike possess the ability to feel pain, to use tools and language, to develop social systems and structures, to seek and grant justice, to empathize, play, love, and mourn.

We do not know if animals have souls, though the Bible tells us that animals worship their Creator and that the whole creation is part of the covenant community. We do know that God came to us in the form of a human who embraced those who were rejected and "otherized" so far out of the bounds of society that they weren't considered human. God served the other, sacrificed for the other, loved the other, without ever not being God. We don't have to reject our humanity to show compassion to animals. Rather, by showing compassion, we are being the best version of humans that we can be.

Volf points out the danger of engaging in black-hole humanity, in assimilating everything and everyone into ourselves: "Vilify all boundaries, pronounce every discrete identity oppressive, put the tag 'exclusion' on every stable difference—and you will have aimless drifting instead of clear-sighted agency, haphazard activity instead of moral engagement and accountability and, in the long run, a torpor of death instead of a dance of freedom."[7] By embracing our identity as human, animals' identity as animal, and our common identity as creatures of God, we better situate ourselves to act as servants to one another and to God, recognizing and acting on the image of God, the author and protector of creation, in ourselves.

The Kingdom of God Is Here, Bearing Hope

> Therefore, if anyone is in Christ, the new creation has come: The old has gone, the new is here! All this is from God, who reconciled us to himself through Christ and gave us the ministry of reconciliation: that God was reconciling the world to himself in Christ, not counting people's sins against them. And he has committed to us the message of reconciliation.
>
> —2 Corinthians 5:17–19

The kingdom of God is a prominent topic in Jesus' recorded teachings. Jesus surprised his followers by declaring that the kingdom of God was among them. And the gospel of Matthew reminds us that the prophet Isaiah foretold the birth of Emmanuel, which means "God with us." So God *literally* is walking in first-century Palestine, and in addition an element of this declaration communicates a future hope, an announcement that what is to come (heaven, the reign of God, the release of humanity from sin) has already begun. Practically, Jesus' declaration must have seemed like a bit of insanity to a people under the thumb of Roman military occupation. The arrival of Jesus on earth, his crucifixion, resurrection, and ascension are the in-breaking of the kingdom of God to earth. All that happens after occurs in a time of "already but not yet." The kingdom is here, but it is not yet fully realized. The kingdom is here, but we see only glimpses. The kingdom is here, pulsing, feeding, growing, living, waiting. The old creation has gone and the new is taking its place.

But what is the kingdom of God? What does it look like? What does Jesus teach us about the kingdom?

- The kingdom requires repentance (Matt. 4:17). But it's a different kind of repentance than the reluctant, mumbled "sorry" we wheedle out of our children, or the sorry-not-sorry we declare after a backhanded compliment. We are to repent from sitting in the shadow of death, to live in light.
- The kingdom requires humility, meekness, righteousness, mercy, peacemaking, obedience, discipleship, reconciliation, love of enemies, generosity, forgiveness, seeking of God, prayer, and faithful action (Matt. 5–7).
- The kingdom is God's will, done on earth as it is in heaven (Matt. 6:10).

- The kingdom is growing among the weeds (Matt. 13:24–25). Kingdom living can start small and grow to protect and provide for all (Matt. 13:31–32). The kingdom is contagious, transforming those it touches into new ways of nourishing, growing, living (Matt. 13:33).

- The kingdom of God doesn't look like earthly kingdoms. It raises up the lowly and puts the last first (Mark 10:31). The kingdom of God puts love before tradition, creative flourishing before rigid legalism (Mark 12:28–34). The kingdom of God is righteousness and peace and joy in the Holy Spirit (Rom. 14:17).

- Things might get rough before they get better (Mark 13:8). The whole creation is groaning for reconciliation with its Creator (Rom. 8:22).

- But the kingdom of God is here, among and within us. We are called to orient ourselves to kingdom living in radical, life-giving ways (Luke 17:33).

- In the kingdom of God, we submit to God and to one another in order to cultivate the "harvest of righteousness and peace" (Heb. 12:11). We pursue peace and reject bitterness (Heb. 12:14–15). We worship, give thanks, show hospitality, live simply, and love generously (Heb. 12:28–13:5).

- You may notice that the kingdom of God looks a lot like life in the body of Christ, in the church, should look, because "the kingdom of the world has become the kingdom of our Lord" (Rev. 11:15).

- Of course, it's not all sunshine and soy lattes. Not yet. Because when the kingdom comes, when we see in full, "death will be no more; mourning and crying and pain will be no more" (Rev. 21:4 NRSV).

What can we learn from these teachings about caring for the earth and its creatures?

First, we can't simply wring our hands and hope for the best. "To take part in God's reconciliation of the world is not to pine after some lost Eden. It is to live in anticipation of the new Jerusalem, the heavenly city come down to earth."[8] Jesus taught us to pray, to pursue God's will "on earth as it is in heaven." We're not to wait; we're to act. More accurately, we are called not to resist the working of the Spirit within us. Reconciled to God, we "must make space for others in ourselves and invite them in—even our enemies."[9] In doing so, we choose to live in a way that is eschatomorphic; we become reshaped by living out the implications of the eschaton, when every knee will bow and every tongue will give praise to the God who created and redeems the world.

Second, a significant mark of the kingdom of God is the renewal of the created world, the reconciliation of *all things* back to their Creator.[10] Heaven will come to us. And the Bible is clear that humans are not alone in this drama of reconciliation. The *whole creation* groans, in part because "the form of life that succeeds by grasping or hoarding or profiteering—abundantly on display in today's food production system and in fast-food eating patterns—is precisely the kind of life that Jesus came to correct through his own example. There is no resurrection life without the self-giving that the cross reveals."[11]

Most of us reading this book probably eat three times a day. Maybe more, maybe less if you're like me and consider black coffee the breakfast of champions. One of the ways the church has always entered into the kingdom of God is through eating, often a central part of fellowship. It's why the discussion of whether or not it was okay to eat food that had been sacrificed to foreign gods was such a dominant topic in the early church writings: they were feeling out the practicalities of extending hospitality to all, of practicing the good news of Jesus Christ with *all*, in light of centuries-long traditions and doctrine. Jesus himself invites us into the body by offering his, which we commemorate each time we take the bread and wine of communion (or a cracker and grape juice if you grew up like me).

The communion meal is significant for those of us who wish to steward creation well, in these three ways: it is simple, it is shared, and it is voluntarily sacrificial. I don't think our eating patterns often conform to this example. As someone who has struggled with food addiction, I have frequently eaten in secret, jamming as much food as I can into my body as quickly as I can. In our culture's quest for cheap food, we create economic and physical structures that sacrifice the lives and well-being of the whole creation: human and animal; land, air, and water. But in participating in communion, we "go to die ourselves. It is the regular time when we learn to put to death all the self-serving impulses that distort and degrade the world around us."[12] Unfortunately, many Christians take the "self-sacrificing" step of calling for more recycling, fewer car rides, and a simpler lifestyle while making other creatures die (and other people kill) for what's on their dinner plates.

Walking With

The wolf will live with the lamb, the leopard will lie down with the goat, the calf and the lion and the yearling together; and a little child will lead them. The cow will feed with the bear, their young will lie down together, and the lion will eat straw like the ox. The infant will play near the cobra's den, the young child will put its hand into the viper's nest. They will neither harm nor destroy on all my holy mountain, for the earth will be filled with the knowledge of the LORD as the waters cover the sea. In that day the Root of

Jesse will stand as a banner for the peoples; the nations will rally to him, and his resting place will be glorious.

—*Isaiah 11:6–10*

Of the accounts of Jesus' forty days in the wilderness, only Mark includes the following words: "He was with the wild animals" (1:13). Growing up in a developed suburban neighborhood, and living now in a major city, I find it pretty easy to gloss over this phrase. Jesus is in the *wilderness*. Of *course* there are wild animals. What's the big deal? But I need to remember what it would have been like for an early Christian to hear the words, and consider that they were chosen carefully.

My first encounter with a "wild" animal was a camel who spit on me at the Boise zoo. I can't blame him. He was probably terribly bored, and I'm sure my reaction provided him a little amusement. The Boise zoo is a hideously depressing place. The enclosures are small and barren, and animals whom God created to roam free ought to be ticked off to be there. Aside from an occasional whale sighting off the Oregon coast, the raccoon mom who made a springtime nursery in one of our backyard trees, and city foxes foraging for food, my knowledge and observation of wild animals have come through television. When I think about wild animals, then, it's from a very distant perspective.

But that's not how a first-century Christian would have considered these words. At that time, sprawl hadn't overtaken so many wildlife habitats. Real-life encounters with wildlife weren't mediated by stone walls and chain-link fences. Yet thanks to the legacy of sin, the animals of the earth feared humans and acted accordingly.

So Jesus really should have been either hiding from the wild animals, protecting himself from them, or showing them who was boss. But Mark says he didn't do any of those things. Jesus simply was *with* the wild animals. Bauckham points out that the

Greek term Mark uses is a positive phrase, often used to indicate friendship and closeness.[13] Jesus didn't just avoid harming the wild animals, or avoid being harmed *by* them; he made creatures commonly believed to be enemies of humans into friends.[14] It calls to mind Isaiah's prophetic kingdom vision of interspecies harmony, a reality that is both Edenic and to come. Bauckham writes:

> [Jesus' peaceable companionship with the animals in the wilderness] . . . gains a new power for modern Christians in a world of ecological destruction. . . . Mark's image of Jesus with the animals provides a Christological warrant for and a biblical symbol of the human possibility of living fraternally with other living creatures, a possibility given by God in creation and given back in messianic redemption. Like all aspects of Jesus' inauguration of the kingdom of God, its fullness will be realized only in the eschatological future, but it can be significantly anticipated in the present.[15]

Not only can this picture of peaceful possibility point Jesus followers toward practices that promote fraternal coexistence with our fellow creatures—it mandates such a response. If we take seriously our call to live into the kingdom now, if it truly is "time to take our humble and responsible place within God's abundant life, in which pain and death will be no more,"[16] should we start by not eating other creatures?

On the cross, God began a reconciling work. Archbishop Desmond Tutu calls it a "centripetal process":

> There is a movement, not easily discernible, at the heart of things to reverse the awful centrifugal force of alienation, brokenness, division, hostility, and disharmony. God has set in motion a centripetal process, a moving toward the center, toward unity, harmony, goodness, peace and justice, a process that removes barriers. Jesus says, "And when I am lifted up from the earth I shall draw everyone to myself" as

he hangs on the cross with outflung arms. Thrown out to clasp all, everyone and everything, in a cosmic embrace, so that all, everyone, everything belongs. None is an outsider, all are insiders, all belong.[17]

This centripetal process starts from the inside out. Volf argues that "the Spirit of God breaks through the self-enclosed worlds we inhabit; the Spirit re-creates us and sets us on the road to becoming . . . a personal microcosm of the eschatological new creation."[18] When we enter into life with Jesus, we die to ourselves, making room for the other. "I have been crucified with Christ and I no longer live, but Christ lives in me. The life I now live in the body, I live by faith in the Son of God, who loved me and gave himself for me" (Gal. 2:20).

Letting our old ways pass away isn't a piece of cake. Often when we speak up against exclusion, we are mocked, or worse. "To refuse to sing and march, to protest the madness of the spectacle, appears irrational and irresponsible, naïve and cowardly, treacherous toward one's own and dangerously sentimental toward the evil enemy."[19] People have accused me of emotionalizing, of being soft on animals. As if love somehow made us weak, not strong. What does it say about our view of God, of our Savior, and of Christianity, if looking on someone with compassion, if choosing to restrain our strength, if choosing mercy over violence are seen as mistakes, as weakness, as dangerous? Gandhi said, "First they ignore you, then they laugh at you, then they fight you, then you win." Paul said it a different way: "For the message of the cross is foolishness to those who are perishing, but to us who are being saved it is the power of God" (1 Cor. 1:18).

Jesus' power is foolish power. God in flesh delivered to die on a cross after living as a social outcast? Crazy. Eating meat, going to the zoo, and wearing leather shoes used to be all I knew. But there's a better way, and the reality of our current use and abuse of animals prompts us to follow it.

Discussion Questions

1. Who are some of the "others" in your life?
2. Think of a time when you loved an "other." What compelled you to act?
3. In what ways are animals a part of your life?
4. How do you consider animals? How have you related to animals today? This week?

PART 2

Using Animals

In the first three chapters, we explored what it means to be made in the image of a Trinitarian God and how that knowledge ought to inform our praxis of stewardship and love. Carefully examining and applying this framework opens paths toward reconciliation with God, with our own conflicted selves, and with God's creation. What I have said in the past few chapters is not news to Jesus followers—I am calling on values and practices that are as old as our faith. What I ask is that we look at the world around us, and specifically at the realities of how animals are treated when they are used by humans for human gain, and ask, "Are these practices compatible with my faith?"

While speaking at a conference on Christian ethics, theologian Reggie Williams said, "The inability to see those furthest down inhibits our ability to practice our faith." Join me as we turn our eyes to God's other creatures.

CHAPTER 4

Animals in Our Homes

Justice, Miss Piggy, Kassy, and Lucy

When Justice was a pup, his owner gave him to a neighbor. Two months later, his original owner called PETA, distraught because the collar she had put on him as a baby had never been removed and was now grown into his skin. When fieldworkers found Justice, he was tied under a deck with only a plastic travel crate to shelter him from the frigid Virginia winter.

For nine years, PETA's fieldworkers visited Miss Piggy. Her owners weren't cruel people, but they completely neglected the dog they kept chained in the back yard, save the one time they attempted to treat her fleas by pouring motor oil on her back. The fieldworkers checked on Miss Piggy every few months, providing flea and tick medicine, toys, clean straw bedding, a sturdy house, a lightweight tie-out to replace her heavy and prone-to-tangle chain, and tummy rubs, which were perhaps what Miss Piggy wanted most of all. On their final visit to the house, they noticed that Miss Piggy, who had always been stocky, had become severely emaciated, all of her ribs clearly visible through her thin skin. A large tumor on her leg had erupted and reeked of infection. She was unable to put weight on the leg and had been vomiting for days. Her owners realized that Miss Piggy was dying and for once thought of her needs, asking the fieldworkers who had given Miss Piggy the only affection she'd ever known to give her a peaceful release from her pain.

In early April 2015, Kassy was removed from a Mechanicsburg, Ohio, breeder along with nearly 140 other dogs. She was so terrified, she quivered at any human touch. Rescuers and law enforcement from multiple jurisdictions were called in to help with the operation and found urine-stained, feces-crusted dogs housed in barren runs without access to water. The breeder pled guilty to *three* counts of cruelty to animals. His punishment included probation, fines, and surrendering his kennel license, but he was allowed to keep five dogs.

On April 7, 2015, wearing gas masks to protect them from noxious fumes and toxic air, volunteers with the Animal Rescue Corps removed more than eighty dogs from a licensed breeding facility in Kankakee County, Illinois. A home breeder voluntarily surrendered the animals, who were found in tiny pens with plastic wire flooring, perched over urine- and feces-soaked cardboard. Suffering from untreated eye infections, respiratory infections, and dental problems as a result of lack of veterinary care, the dogs greeted volunteers with ears pressed flat to their heads, many terrified of the slightest human touch. A few days after her rescue from this hellhole, Lucy, a tiny red Chihuahua, gave birth to her final litter of puppies, who, thanks to the rescuers, would be spared their mother's sad life of breeding litter upon litter.

I've told four stories about dogs here, but I could easily tell four stories about cats, rabbits, hamsters, birds, or any of the other animals that humans have domesticated and now breed and sell for profit. Though comparatively few animals are bred as pets, dogs and cats are often the animals with whom we have the closest relationships. Many of us share homes with one or more pets and love them. This chapter briefly discusses the basics of breeding animals as pets, some moral objections to a billion-dollar pet industry, and the questions that arise when we love some animals and use others as food.

Great Expectations

When I was growing up, all of my family's pets came from breeders. Maybe a friend's dog had a litter, or we wanted a specific breed, so we found the closest breeder who sold puppies of that specific kind. We weren't wealthy by any means, so purchase prices were always modest. Pet shops charged too much, and the dogs and cats inside often looked a bit lethargic or runny-nosed, so we looked for ads in the newspaper or just asked around.

Like most folks who don't know better, we assumed that if we wanted a dog or a cat, we needed to go to a pet store or breeder, particularly if we were looking for specific traits. Our dogs lived inside with us, but my uncle, who lived on a farm, kept his outside or in the garage. Today, I have many friends who adhere to the "adopt, don't shop" motto when it comes to adding animals to their homes, but just as many who seek out breeders for specific animals. The ones who buy cite reasons such as wanting to know exactly what kind of dog they are getting when they buy; or claim that a puppy mill is different from a responsible breeder; or say that adoption is great but just isn't for them.

The Billion-Dollar Pet Industry

Dogs, cats, and other animals have become victims of our consumer culture. Upwards of eight million dogs and cats are surrendered to shelters each year in the United States. That's more than 913 animals every hour being dumped or dropped at local humane societies and city pounds. Ask someone who works in intake at one of these shelters why people are giving up their animals:

- He barks too much.
- She doesn't bark enough. I need a guard dog.

- She was cute as a puppy, but now she's too big.
- He's too small.
- He chews.
- She's not playful enough.
- He's too old.
- She's too young.
- I don't have time to house-train him.
- She digs.
- I'm moving.
- My apartment doesn't allow cats.
- I'm allergic.
- I'm pregnant.
- My new girlfriend doesn't like him.

I live in the city of Philadelphia, where the Animal Care and Control Team (ACCT) contracts with the city to provide shelter and care for the city's homeless and abandoned animals. More than twenty-eight thousand animals per year pass through the doors of the shelter, which is open twenty-four hours a day, seven days a week, every day of the year. In the last five days of January 2013, ACCT took in more than 175 dogs, presumably many who were Christmas gifts from whom the shine had worn off. Over Memorial Day weekend that same year, the shelter took in 125 cats and kittens. In one weekend. In March 2015, the shelter took in 1,740 animals, 677 of whom were surrendered by their owners. Of the 711 dogs brought in that month, 339 were surrendered by their owners.[1]

Here are some of the comments (complete with language and terrible spelling and grammar) you can read in the review sections of various ACCT Facebook pages:

- "I had to take my 7 month old puppy pitbull there she wasn't ficious [sic] she just needed that one person who had the time for her energy and like any puppy they can't be left in a crate all day. . . . we dropped her off on a Friday gave it until that Monday to see how she was doing and those MF put my dog down." *Translation:* I bought a puppy without understanding how much time and energy it takes to care for a puppy properly. Now I'm blaming the shelter for my guilty conscience.

- "We put our dog there. He never got to get in the system at all. They killed him in less than 24 hours. It kills me to see that a nice dog who was scared and acting up had to be put down. If ie [*sic*] would have known that i would have never had the dog go there. 5 years i had him and out of no where i find out he is put down. . . . And just cuz i put him there does not mean i killed him." *Translation:* My confused and terrified dog, whose life was totally upended when I abandoned him after five years, was euthanized. And even though I gave up all my rights to guardianship as soon as I handed over the leash, I'm blaming the shelter for my decision.

- "I work 7 days a week, my boyfriend is a full-time student. I recently bought a puppy. . . . He had heart worms . . . and being away from his mom he wasn't eating right. . . . So my boyfriend and I made the hardest decision of our life . . . to 'SURRENDER' OUR pup to ACCT. We had to let him go because we wouldn't have time to care for him. . . . Later in the after noon i told my boyfriend to call them. He did and they said he have 'PASSED' away." *Translation:* I bought a puppy, even though I don't have time to care for a dog. When my puppy got sick, I surrendered him to a shelter, where he was euthanized because of his illness. But I blame the shelter.

- "This year, Americans were projected to spend $350 million on Halloween costumes for their pets. Meanwhile Ariel will probably be put to death tomorrow, Nov 1 because ACCT does not have the means to help with her dental disease, requiring extractions." *Translation:* I understand how this system works and hope to urge you to do something to make it better.

A neighborhood friend of mine was waiting in ACCT for her foster dog to come out when she witnessed a woman bring a dog to intake because she was "tired of him" and then ask to see the dogs available for adoption.

The stories in my neighborhood are the same as stories in Chicago, Baltimore, Los Angeles, Portland, Kansas City, and all around the country. How did we get here?

The blame for overpopulation lies at the feet of breeders and buyers. But breeding and buying are a symptom of an infection of self, of sin, that affects us all and that has been infecting our minds and hearts since sin entered into the world.

Breeders

There are between two and three thousand USDA-licensed dog-breeding facilities in the United States in any given year, but not all breeders are required to have a license. The American Society for the Prevention of Cruelty to Animals (ASPCA) estimates that there are ten thousand breeding mills in the United States, with the number of dogs at each mill varying wildly, from ten to well over one thousand.[2] Under federal law, dogs in these facilities are required cage space no more than six inches beyond their body size in all directions and cages can be stacked on top of one another, allowing urine and feces to fall through to dogs and cages below.[3] The most stringent state law in the country requires twice the federal space (so, twelve inches wider than the dog in any direction). This most stringent state law also requires access to the outdoors and annual veterinary exams and prohibits wire cages and the stacking of cages.[4] In other words, the most stringent state law provides the bare minimum standard of decent care.

ASPCA research indicates that nationwide, nearly 30 percent of dogs are purchased from breeders and about an equal percentage of cats and dogs are adopted from shelters and rescues.[5] Older data from breeding enthusiasts put the number of dogs obtained from breeders at a higher rate: 31 percent from show breeders, 23 percent from backyard breeders, and 7 percent from pet stores, with the remaining dogs being of "mixed breed."[6]

Money fuels the pet industry, whether we're talking about dogs and cats or hamsters and frogs. And when money fuels, obedience to God can fall by the wayside. It's why Jesus drove the money changers and merchants out of the temple.

While puppy mills receive a lot of media attention, the plight of small animals in the pet industry goes largely unnoticed, but their lives are generally misery from the start. Undercover investigations have revealed hamsters and other small animals bred in filthy warehouses. Sick animals are often left to suffer or thrown into freezers to die slowly or tossed into bags and bashed against a hard surface. The animals who survive are bought and shipped to pet stores in bulk, much like any other commodity. It's a profit-driven system with little regard for the needs and welfare of the animals on whom it depends, since a single life has no impact on the bottom line.

Undercover investigations at breeding facilities of dogs, cats, hamsters, mice, frogs—any animal we have domesticated and share our homes with—have found horrific abuses at every level of the supply chain, from breeders to transport centers to the pet stores that sell animals for profit. Employees of these facilities are often untrained and animals frequently lack access to basic necessities and veterinary care. Sick and suffering animals languish until they die, or they are killed by crude and cruel methods. The God-given instincts of animals are rarely met. Hamsters, for instance, are largely solitary creatures. At the homes of pet breeders and in pet shops, however, they are forced to live in close quarters with dozens of other hamsters. One pet shop I visited in Alabama kept row upon row of hamsters in clear plastic cages, with the barest layer of newspaper as bedding. Since hamsters love to burrow deep as protection from predators, some of the hamsters attempted to fight through the plastic. One raised himself on his back legs and tried frantically to climb out of the cage, again and again and again.

Buyers and the Illness That Breeds Them

Even though we euthanize three to four million animals in US shelters each year, breeders continue to breed because buyers continue to buy. And while the breed/buy/surrender cycle costs taxpayers two billion dollars annually,[7] year after year the pet products industry rakes in billions of dollars. In 2015, the estimated revenue for the pet industry, the total amount that Americans spent on their pets, was over sixty billion dollars. The Food and Agriculture Organization of the United Nations estimates that it would take *thirty* billion dollars to eradicate world hunger.[8] I'm not making this comparison to condemn those who take in and care for homeless animals—I share my own home with dogs and cats and probably always will. I am merely pointing out that breeding and buying animals is big business.

Some municipalities have recognized that one step toward curbing pet overpopulation—reducing the number of healthy and adoptable animals who are euthanized because shelters run out of space—is to implement breeding restrictions or mandatory spay and neuter laws. Because these laws threaten profits, breeders fight them tooth and nail. It is critical that those of us who choose to share our homes with animals spay and neuter them, and encourage everyone we know to do the same. Doing so is a responsible exercise of our stewardship of God's creation in a world where millions of domesticated animals are abused, homeless, and abandoned.

My family and I give away our things regularly. Our church community hosts free baby and kids' goods exchanges, at which folks drop off and pick up their gently used gear, clothes, and toys. There's no charge; it's just an opportunity to meet new friends and share in God's abundance. I might feel a twinge of nostalgia putting a favorite toy or stuffed animal in the giveaway box. Or I might feel a different sort of twinge when I toss into the thrift store box that pair of pants that will probably never fit again. The feeling doesn't run deep, because these things are just that—things.

Animals aren't things. They're not commodities that we should toss away when they're no longer convenient. Nor should they be considered business assets or profit-generating machines. Animals are made by God; God delights in them and cares for them. God watches over them, and they respond in worship and service. Anyone who shares a home with an animal can tell you that they have individual personalities, quirks, likes, dislikes, and ways of communicating. And this goes far beyond the dogs and cats whom we primarily think of as pets. Rats, for instance, are extraordinarily intelligent and communicative animals who love to play and desire affection.

But the pet industry too often treats animals like things, not only in its commodification of their bodies to fuel corporate profits but also in its treatment of the animals themselves.

As a child and teenager, I didn't treat the animals in my family's care with the respect they were due as creatures of God. When our young lab puppy peed in the house, I hit her on the face with a rolled-up newspaper. When I wanted my cockapoo to go faster on our walks, or to slow down, or if I was having a bad day, I yanked the leash so the choke-chain got her attention and showed her who was boss. She weighed fifteen pounds. When I first adopted a cat, I cleaned out her litter box only when the smell got to be too much for *me* to handle, never mind her delicate nose and paws.

Legal protections prohibiting cruelty to animals exist in every state and the District of Columbia, serving as a "morality" clause to punish people who are caught acting too far out of bounds.[9] Anti-cruelty laws are good. In the Old Testament, God included the care of animals in the laws given to the Israelites. Most of today's laws prohibit people from intentionally abandoning an animal or exposing an animal to danger, lack of shelter, lack of food, and so on. I think it's appropriate that every state can now prosecute cruelty to animals as a felony.[10] But the problem of cruelty to animals can't be legislated out of existence. We also must address the spiritual sickness that causes cruelty.

Symptoms

The commodification and objectification of animal life have consequences that reach far beyond pet shop doors. Violence toward animals and violence toward humans are the fruit of the same sick tree.

Study after study shows that people who are violent to animals in childhood go on to be violent to others in their lives. Here are just a few examples of recent findings:

- "Violent offenders were significantly more likely than nonviolent offenders to have committed acts of cruelty toward pet animals as children."[11]

- "[Of 307 men arrested for domestic violence,] forty-one percent ($n = 125$) of the men committed at least one act of animal abuse since the age of 18, in contrast to the 1.5 percent prevalence rate reported by men in the general population."[12]
- "Based on survey data from 180 inmates at a medium- and maximum-security prison in a Southern state, the present study examines the relationship between the demographic characteristics of race, level of education, the residential location of an offender's formative years, and recurrent acts of childhood cruelty [toward animals] and their impact on later repeated acts of interpersonal violence. *Only* repeated acts of animal cruelty during childhood was predictive of later recurrent acts of violence toward humans."[13]
- "Those who were above the median with regard to both victimization and perpetration of physical bullying exhibited the highest rates of involvement in multiple acts of animal abuse and also exhibited the lowest levels of sensitivity with regard to cruelty-related attitudes pertaining to animals."[14]

The Bible also makes this connection between violence to animals and people. On his deathbed, Jacob notes that "Simeon and Levi are brothers—their swords are weapons of violence. Let me not enter their council, let me not join their assembly, for they have killed men in their anger and hamstrung oxen as they pleased. Cursed be their anger, so fierce, and their fury, so cruel!" (Gen. 49:5–7). You'll recall that Simeon and Levi were the brothers who together killed every male in the city in which their sister Dinah was raped.

The spiritual sickness that allows one person to oppress another, whether through violence or other means, stems from the disease of sin, of believing that might makes right, of believing that *I* am worthier and more deserving than *you*. It is the same twisted thinking, the dangerous dream that we can be "like God," that first shattered the harmony of Eden. Instead of conforming ourselves to God's image, we imagine ourselves to be God-like in power and authority, forgetting that when God took on human flesh in Jesus, his life was one of service and sacrifice.

Sacrifice

Imagine if we viewed our relationship with the animals in our homes as a sacrificial one instead of one modeled after owner and object. As a young adult, I started to see and treat the dogs and cats in my home as individuals who needed to express their cat-ness and dog-ness, who had needs that might not conform to my desires.

Sometimes this was simple. Max the cat needed to scratch to keep her claws trimmed. At first, I got angry at her for using the window screens and my favorite chair. Then my mom and I made a glorious cat tree out of wood and rope we bought at a local hardware store, and I moved the chair to a room she couldn't access.

I adopted another cat, Katie, who liked to secretly urinate in places that weren't the litter box. Then I read that cats are very fastidious and clean animals, who will never urinate in the same place twice in the wild. I was expecting her to share a rarely cleaned box with another cat. I purchased a second litter box and scooped them out twice a day, an extra minute of work for me, and she stopped leaving secret pees in the house.

When my husband and I adopted Clyde as a six-month-old puppy, he'd already been bounced from home to home at least five times. He was a wreck. He panicked every time we left the house, taking his worry out on the floors and furniture. We had three options: give up and give him away, put him in a crate when we weren't home, or show him patience and love. We chose the latter. Instead of forcing him into a wire crate for hours on end, which only would have exacerbated his fears, we gated him into the kitchen and dining room, where he could cause only minimal damage but still have room to walk around and access to look outside. We didn't always keep our cool. One afternoon I came home to let Clyde out for lunch, and he crawled under the back deck and wouldn't come out. I was stressed, late for a meeting back at the office, and angry. No wonder he wasn't keen on leaving his hiding spot. He was bored at home alone all day; he wanted freedom, fresh air, and someone to play with. We started to better understand that dogs are pack animals and adopted sweet Emma, with whom he could cuddle and play all day.

I drive home at lunch to let the dogs out of the house because I know that dogs love to spend a bit of time in the back yard and need to be let out to relieve themselves in the middle of the day. It's a restorative break for me and I see the appreciation on their faces and in their bodies as they rush into the yard for their midday adventure.

Saying Goodbye

If you've cared for an animal through death, you know it's a sacrificial commitment, both financially and emotionally. Because our commitment to the animals in our home is lifelong, it means that we suffer loss regularly. And it means that we sometimes have to make the decision to end our beloved pet's suffering, even if we're not ready to say goodbye.

It means I had to tell my five-year-old son that our sweet dog

Emma was too sick to save and would need to be euthanized, and hold him while he wailed in my arms as I, too, sobbed at the unexpected and wrenching decision we'd had to make far too soon. It meant that when we picked Isaiah up from the friends who watched him while we euthanized our elderly cat Max, I watched his young face fall when he saw her now-empty cat carrier, the reality of what we had done having finally sunk in. We'll go through these same painful steps at least four more times in the coming years. It will never get easier or less painful.

A friend of mine was struggling with the decision to end his beloved companion dog's life. At sixteen years old, her quality of life had declined significantly. He had a reasonable question: "Shouldn't God be the one to decide when she dies?"

I say that commodification and cruelty come from an impulse to act "like God," but is that the same impulse that allows us to give our pets a merciful release from suffering? Perhaps. Yet it hurts us to exercise this power far more than it hurts them. A brief pinprick of the needle is followed by a peaceful release, a quick and painless end of the disease or pain that has wracked their bodies. To me, being held by us while a veterinarian administers humane euthanasia is the final gift we can give to the companions who bring us joy and help us develop into more patient, loving, and caring individuals. In the last year, I have held two animals in my arms as they have slipped away, caressing their fur and faces, whispering and singing into their ears, assuring them that I would never forget the sweetness and joy they brought into my life, telling them that they had served well.

It wasn't *me* they had served, ultimately. They served God. By being their dog and cat selves, they had shown me how to be more merciful, more loving, and more compassionate, centered not on my own wants and needs but on the needs of others. Their lives pointed to God and directed me toward God as well. Even if they had never interacted with a human, their lives would have glorified God. God would have seen them, and they would have seen and responded to God. "How many are your works, LORD! In wisdom you made them all; the earth is full of your creatures" (Ps. 104:24).

The Scriptures repeatedly remind us that there is one God, who is in and through all creation. Each of us has a part to play in the drama of life. Ours as humans is not to dominate or subsume the lives of animals but rather to allow them to flourish so that they may play their part as well.

Discussion Questions

1. If you share your home with a companion, consider life from their perspective. What comes up? Are there any changes you can make to create space and opportunity for them to flourish more fully?

2. What are some ways we objectify and commodify animals? Are there benefits for animals? Dangers for humans?

3. Recall a time in your life when you've treated an animal with less respect or patience or love than we are called to. What caused that?

CHAPTER 5

Animals in (and out of) the Wild

Tony, Karen, and Lolita

Tony was six months old when he was purchased. Though more than a dozen other tigers have come and gone over the fifteen years since his initial purchase, the 550-pound Tony now spends his days alone in a forty-by-eighty-foot enclosure, breathing the exhaust of idling eighteen-wheelers and diesel fuel, just another on the list of attractions including a twenty-four-hour restaurant and gift shop at a truck stop in rural Louisiana. Tony's concrete-block den is adjacent to a grassy patch and a small pool. Photos show the occasional ball, but not much else to provide entertainment or stimulation during the long days and nights confined to his cage. In the wild, Siberian tigers live in hilly forests and are highly mobile, traveling hundreds of miles in their lifetimes. They are agile and active animals, always on the move. Though he was bred, born, and raised in captivity, the thick steel bars, the high fence topped with barbed wire, and the steel grid roof of the enclosure betray the fact that Tony, like all other tigers, is wild at heart.

Karen was born in Thailand in 1969. When she was still nursing, she was forcefully removed from her mother and extended family and shipped around the world to be trained to perform in the Ringling Brothers circus. She was trained the way all baby elephants are trained by Ringling: roped, beaten with a bullhook, and whipped until she complied with the trainer's demands. For more than four decades, Karen has spent day after day chained in a boxcar, being carted from one performance to another, forced to stand and sleep in her own waste. She bobs and sways almost nonstop, as animals in captivity often do, a sign that they are bored, depressed, and distressed. Karen has tested positive for tuberculosis antibodies and suffers from severe foot problems. Foot disease is the number one killer of captive elephants, because God didn't design elephants to stand in one spot for days—or even hours—at a time, as Ringling forces their elephants to do. She has a noticeable scar on her jawline from where a handler hit her with a bullhook and it sank so deep into her flesh that he had trouble removing it.

In the wild, female elephants stay with their extended families for their entire lives. Elephants are social and intelligent animals, forming strong bonds with one another. They grieve when a loved one dies and make pilgrimages to their bones for years afterward. They can make tools and speak to one another across great distances. They are fiercely protective of and loyal to their families, and they roam for miles and miles in herds, covering up to one hundred miles in a single day, foraging for food. The elephants used for Ringling Brothers and other circuses and traveling acts are denied every one of their natural longings and needs. In the barns where Ringling breeds baby elephants to add to its traveling shows, mother elephants give birth while they are roped, forced to stand in the same spot, unable to move to relieve the pain of labor. Their babies are immediately taken from them as they wail and strain against the chains that hold them in place.

Lolita was four years old when she was taken from her pod, one of dozens of orcas captured from the same group between 1965 and 1973, each delivered to a marine park for display. Of the orcas captured during that time, she is the only one still living. Marine biologists believe that Lolita's mother, now in her eighties, is still alive and swimming with the very pod from which Lolita was stolen. For a few years, Lolita shared her tiny tank at the Miami Seaquarium with a male orca named Hugo. But in 1980, after more than a decade of confinement, Hugo bashed his head against the concrete wall of his tank again and again until he died. Lolita, an orca whom God made to be with other orcas, has been alone ever since, performing twice a day.

In the wild, orcas swim an average of eighty miles per day. Lolita's tank measures just eighty feet by thirty-five feet. The water is twenty feet deep. Lolita is twenty-two feet long.

Lolita may be the loneliest orca in captivity, but she isn't the last. SeaWorld Parks in the United States also keep social, intelligent, and highly mobile orcas in concrete tanks. Corky, an orca at SeaWorld San Diego, has lived in captivity for nearly half a century. Corky and Lolita have lived in tanks for longer than I've been alive.

For hundreds, even thousands of years, humans have captured wild animals and used them for entertainment or sport. We have taken animals out of the homes God created for them and put them on display in zoos, circuses, and aquariums. We have too often ignored the presence of animals and bulldozed their habitats in order to build shopping malls and housing developments. In the Amazon rain forests, millions of acres of habitat have been burned in order to plant crops to feed to cattle raised for meat. While hunting animals for food was once considered necessary for survival, today "canned" and "trophy" hunts are common. In this chapter, we will look at some of the ways humans are stewarding or failing to steward wild animal populations.

Extinction and Captivity

> How long will the land lie parched and the grass in every
> field be withered? Because those who live in it are wicked,
> the animals and birds have perished.
>
> —*Jeremiah 12:4*

Since 2006, 121 species have gone extinct.[1] Largely because
of human activity, 121 types of unique, God-created animals
have been eliminated.[2] Endangered Species International cites
five main causes of the current alarming rate of extinction: loss
of habitat, including from the effects of increased greenhouse
gases and other factors of climate change; invasive species, often
the result of human interference in local ecosystems; a rapidly
increasing human population; pollution caused by human activities; and overharvesting (i.e., overfishing and overhunting).[3]

This extinction rate points to a dominion problem. Too
often we are failing in an irreversible way to "till and keep,"
following instead a "haste to make waste" philosophy.

Similarly, zoos and traveling circuses represent a misguided
effort to give ordinary people access to the wonders of the
animal world. Zoos are stocked with animals taken from their
natural habitats, removed from the wild and from the existence
for which God created them, separated from their families and
from the soil and air and water of their birth, and shipped in
crates to fill cages and boxcars around the globe. We may believe
these displays are educational and valuable, but in reality many
exist to generate profits for the companies and entities that run
them. SeaWorld, for instance—which repeatedly and vigorously
touts its conservation efforts—has contributed less than a tiny
fraction of 1 percent of its profits to rescue and rehabilitation
efforts in the last decade.[4]

When baby animals are born in captivity, ticket sales increase.

But those babies grow up, get bigger, and become restless. Baby tigers used for photo ops are taken from their mothers shortly after birth. Federal law allows infant tigers to be handled by the public when they are between eight and twelve weeks old. To ensure a constant supply of tiger cubs in this profitable age range, the breeding continues. But after twelve weeks, the tiger cubs' usefulness has expired, and they are generally shipped to roadside zoos or warehouses until the end of their lives. This sad story is experienced by many animal species unlucky enough to be of value to the "entertainment" industry, including primates used for film and television.

Animals Used for Entertainment

While Ringling Brothers was once able to capture and import elephants from the wild for traveling shows, a change to the Endangered Species Act in the mid-1970s dried up the wild-caught Asian elephant pipeline. So in the mid-1990s Ringling opened a Center for Elephant Conservation, the primary purpose of which was to breed elephants for use in shows. While the Center boasts births of baby elephants, notably absent from its list of elephants born through the years are Ricardo, Benjamin, Kenny, and Bertha—elephants born into Ringling's care who died as babies because of neglect or abuse.

Ringling's website claims that elephants used in traveling acts are provided with round-the-clock veterinary care. Yet three-year-old Kenny refused to eat or drink and was forced to perform even though he was visibly ill. A circus veterinarian finally examined Kenny after two shows and recommended the young elephant be given a break from performing that evening, citing concerns that the public would be disturbed if they saw Kenny bleeding from his rectum (as he had been all day). The elephant trainer overruled the veterinarian and pushed Kenny through a third show. His bloody body was found dead, chained inside the concrete stall where he had been left, just a few hours later.

Ringling's website once claimed their elephants are provided with a clean place to live and scheduled stops during long train rides.[5] Yet according to documents obtained in the course of a lengthy court battle between animal protection organizations and Feld Entertainment, which owns Ringling Brothers, out of six hundred trips over eight years, only fourteen included rest stops. The average travel segment for an elephant on a Ringling tour was twenty-six hours, with travel legs extending to seventy and even one hundred hours straight. Elephants are huge animals who produce correspondingly huge amounts of urine and feces. Though the train cars are equipped with drains, former circus workers have described the overpowering stench they encountered when they opened the elephant car after a journey.[6]

Ringling also claims to welcome regulation. Perhaps that is because the USDA has repeatedly failed to enforce its own requirements. A yearlong *Mother Jones* investigation revealed deep-seated fear of Feld Entertainment, Ringling's parent company, into the upper echelons of federal regulatory agencies. This is not news to the animal protection movement, which has been releasing undercover footage of trainers beating, whipping, and electroshocking elephants, lions, and tigers for decades. More and more members of the public are outraged, as evidenced by ever-decreasing show attendance, but up to this point the USDA has taken no meaningful action. While whistle-blowers have come forward with shocking images of baby-elephant training, Ringling so far has suffered only the lightest of wrist taps.

It's true that the USDA's Animal and Plant Health Inspection Service—the agency in charge of inspections at breeding, experimentation, and entertainment facilities—has limited staff, a little over one hundred employees with nearly nine thousand facilities to monitor, but even egregious cases, like the death of Kenny, go virtually unnoticed by the agency. One former head of APHIS said, "You don't take on an organization like Feld Entertainment without having strong evidence to support it."[7] As a result, though the USDA has "conducted more than a dozen investigations of Feld Entertainment,"[8] it wasn't until late in 2011 that Feld was finally cited for alleged violations of the Animal Welfare Act over a four-year period and forced to pay $270,000 in fines.[9]

The *Mother Jones* investigation found that "Ringling elephants spend most of their long lives either in chains or on trains, under constant threat of the bullhook, or ankus—the menacing tool used to control elephants. They are lame from balancing their 8,000-pound frames on tiny tubs and from being confined in cramped spaces, sometimes for days at a time. They are afflicted with tuberculosis and herpes, potentially deadly diseases rare in the wild and linked to captivity."[10] Is that good stewardship or the careful exercise of dominion?

Shirley was born at Ringling's breeding center in 1995. Traumatized by witnessing the drowning death of another young elephant, she became unwilling or unable to perform and was returned to the breeding center, where she was pregnant before her seventh birthday, well before puberty and at half the age elephants begin to birth their own babies in the wild. During labor, Shirley "was chained by three legs and surrounded by human handlers, who poked her with bullhooks. . . . When the slippery newborn dropped, trainers whisked him away."[11] I saw video footage of this birth. Shirley strained hard against the chains, reaching for her new baby, her whole body probably aching to be near him. This is how God made mother elephants to *be*. They love their babies and want to protect them.

Ringling Brothers is just one example of how a circus uses animals to turn a profit. Other circuses, including UniverSoul, Have Trunk Will Travel, Cole Brothers, Kelly Miller, Shrine, and more are equally guilty of failing to provide adequate care for the animals they use to sell tickets and get buyers in seats.[12]

In a battle between animal welfare and profitability, money generally wins the day.

Until, that is, the circus's public relations machines can no longer stay ahead of reality. That's what is happening to SeaWorld, whose stock price tanked when attendance dropped off after the release of the damning documentary, *Blackfish*.[13]

Killer whales, or orcas, are social and highly mobile animals who communicate with each other through a complex system of pulses and calls and who rely on underwater sound for navigation and orientation. They form matriarchal pods and strong bonds with one another. They are most abundant in cold-water regions, though they can be found in warmer waters as well. Orcas in the wild live to between fifty and one hundred years.[14]

Orcas are protected under the Marine Mammal Protection Act, which was passed in 1972 as a means to protect marine mammals from depletion, the threat of which became real as a result of the hunting and capturing of marine mammals for display. In the late 1970s, SeaWorld and its primary whale hunter were banned from capturing whales in Puget Sound after the hunter's techniques were documented and scrutinized by a public increasingly wary of marine mammal capture.[15]

So, like Ringling, SeaWorld began breeding and sometimes bending the rules in order to introduce new orcas into its programs. The breeding is conducted via artificial insemination with sperm collected by forcing animals to ejaculate. Thirty-seven orcas—whom we know of—died at SeaWorld between 1971 and 2013. None died of old age. Is this the life God intended for orcas when God first created them?

After *Blackfish*, public scrutiny of SeaWorld increased, and so did lawsuits against the company. One such suit uncovered veterinary records and concluded that "orcas at SeaWorld are given psychotropic drugs to stop them from acting aggressively towards each other in the stressful, frustrating conditions in which they're confined instead of funding the development of coastal sanctuaries—the only humane solution."[16]

No matter the façade—whether it's the slick marketing campaigns of corporate behemoths like SeaWorld and Ringling Brothers or a roadside zoo using a dilapidated wooden sign to tout its menagerie of sickly wild animals—the underside of animals in the entertainment industry remains the same: wild animals are taken from the homes God created for them and placed in man-made confinement, often accompanied by poor treatment. Humans "play God" in many ways within the animal kingdom; using animals for entertainment is one of the most obvious yet also one of the most widely accepted.

Zoos

Zoos have always been an ill-conceived way of protecting and enjoying animals,[17] but now we're stuck with facilities full of animals who probably wouldn't have a chance of surviving in the wild. So what to do?

Some zoos have done a fine job making the best of a bad situation. They don't breed animals for the sake of increasing ticket sales or having a photo of a new baby panda to put on their annual brochure. They expand habitats and try to provide the best living arrangements possible for the animals in their care. They accept and provide homes for animals rescued from worse situations. They recognize when they aren't doing a good job with a particular species and move those animals to specially designed sanctuaries.

Other zoos are little more than concrete warehouses, failing to provide for even the most basic of animals' needs. Mali was captured from the wild as a baby the year before I was born.

This elephant, whom God made to love and be cared for by her mother, has lived in a concrete pen at the Manila Zoo for more than three decades. In that time, she's not had contact with a single other elephant. Across the globe, in the Edmonton Valley Zoo, an elephant named Lucy has endured a similar isolated existence.

Most zoos claim "conservation" as their goal, but since habitat loss due to human activity is one of the primary drivers of species extinction, it makes little to no sense to believe that breeding animals in captivity will somehow reverse the trend toward extinction. The World Wildlife Fund points out that captive breeding for the purpose of conservation

> is exceedingly difficult and must be part of a scientifically-based management plan for the species, working closely with the range country government authorities. It is also expensive, and should not be seen as a substitute for in-situ efforts, except in rare circumstances. Captive situations may interfere with the behavioural development of animals by removing them from natural predators and prey. Furthermore, having captive populations of animals does not solve underlying problems of habitat destruction, which are often one of the key causes of the species' decline.[18]

I don't take my son to zoos. When his class schedules a field trip to our local zoo, we stay home and find a different activity. Taking him to a place that subverts God's best for animals—a place that is a pale reflection of the world God created for them—seems a poor way to teach him about the amazing diversity and power of God's creation, and how important it is to care well for our planet and all its inhabitants.[19] Indeed, it's similar to the message we send our children when we teach them to love and be kind to animals while serving them animal parts for dinner. But that's a different chapter!

Hunting

I was born in Idaho and raised in Oregon. My grandfathers hunted. My uncles hunted. My brother hunted. When I lived in Virginia, many of my friends' husbands and fathers hunted. According to the US Fish and Wildlife report of 2011, about 13.7 million Americans hunted that year (or about 4.4 percent of the population).[20]

Let me say this: it isn't necessary for most people in the United States to kill another creature to be able to eat or thrive, and unnecessary killing contradicts our charge to pursue a world "on earth as it is in heaven." *But*. If the only meat a person eats comes from an animal they killed quickly and used every part of, that person is ahead of most of us. When I ate meat, you couldn't have paid me enough money to slaughter and butcher any of the animals I ingested. That was a form of hypocrisy—if I was unwilling to participate in the acts necessary to produce the food I ate, how righteous was I to pay people to do work I couldn't bring myself to do?

That's not how most folks hunt, though. The majority of the small percentage of Americans who hunt do it for fun. In a national survey, only a quarter of hunters killed animals for meat. The other 75 percent hunted "for recreation" or "to be close to nature."[21] Many outdoor activities, including hiking, photography, kayaking, and bird-watching, allow participants to be close to nature. And how ironic is it that killing can be counted as "re-creation"? Creation in the biblical account is about new life, flourishing, and harmony among humans, animals, and the land. Hunting is about conquering.

To be clear, the kind of hunting I'm discussing here is the old-fashioned, take-your-gun-out-into-the-forest-and-walk-around-trying-to-find-tracks-and-maybe-go-home-empty-handed kind. There are those who participate in "canned hunts" or "trophy hunting," and from a "till and keep" perspective there's little nuance there. It's wrong for (usually) rich folks to pay big bucks to visit a farm in Texas or a hunting park in Africa to stalk and slaughter animals with no merciful or life-giving purpose. Have you seen photos of families posing with dead giraffes? Giraffes, who are vegetarian and extremely docile. People pay tens of thousands of dollars to go kill them, $3,000 of which is a "trophy fee." They pay a $35,000 trophy fee to hunt a leopard or cheetah at some parks in South Africa. Or $2,000 for a porcupine.[22] If you prefer a domestic experience and have a little under $10,000 to spare, you can head to places like the Texas Hunt Lodge, where they keep herds of animals on their properties and allow "hunters" of all ages, experiences, and abilities to shoot and kill a variety of species. Take a look at their web page and the expressions on the faces of dead red sheep.[23] Recently I read about an American dentist who allegedly paid guides $55,000 to lure a protected lion off of public land in Zimbabwe, then shot and killed him with a crossbow. Not very sporting behavior.[24]

Rant over. I'm not talking about that kind of hunting.

Some hunters and the state agencies that make money from selling hunting licenses claim that hunting is necessary for population control of certain wild animals. They argue that hunters help maintain symbiosis of local ecosystems by ensuring that animal populations remain healthy and sustainable. But trophy hunting, killing bucks for their antlers, actually increases the size of deer herds.[25] To reduce herd sizes, we have to kill Bambi's mom, not bucks. In addition, the practices of state wildlife management agencies have been shown to artificially boost deer populations,[26] which results in the sale of more hunting licenses (and in higher profits).[27]

There are other options. Without allowing hunting, we could make greater efforts to avoid practices that deplete wildlife habitats and animal population levels would maintain themselves naturally.[28] The connection is clear: we have created a system in which encroachment on and destruction of wildlife habitats disrupt natural ecosystems. Wildlife management agencies receive funding to maintain animal populations to allow hunting to continue in these flawed conditions. Because hunting (and the commerce that comes along with it) is big business, it's all too easy to construct narratives to justify it. Sound familiar? It's the same kind of justification that is at the root of all exclusion discussed in chapter 3.

Yeah, but . . . Animals Are Ours

You don't have to read far into the Bible to see that God and the biblical writers had a deep appreciation for wildlife. Or to see that animals are not ours, they're God's.

- "The earth is the LORD's, and everything in it, the world, and all who live in it" (Ps. 24:1).
- "But ask the animals, and they will teach you, or the birds in the sky, and they will tell you; or speak to the earth, and it will teach you, or let the fish in the sea inform you. Which of all these does not know that the hand of the LORD has done this?" (Job 12:7–9).
- "Do you know when the mountain goats give birth? Do you watch when the doe bears her fawn?" (Job 39:1, and all the rest of Job 39).
- "For every animal of the forest is mine, and the cattle on a thousand hills. I know every bird in the mountains, and the insects in the fields are mine" (Ps. 50:10–11).

All of Psalm 104 is an anthem to the Creator God, who still actively cares for the precious earth: "He makes springs pour water into the ravines; it flows between the mountains. They give water to all the beasts of the field; the wild donkeys quench their thirst. The birds of the sky nest by the waters; they sing among the branches. . . . He makes grass grow for the cattle, and plants for people to cultivate—bringing forth food from the earth" (Ps. 104:10–12, 14).

God provides: "He provides food for the cattle and for the young ravens when they call. His pleasure is not in the strength of the horse, nor his delight in the legs of the warrior" (Ps. 147:9–10). God provides for the purpose of providing, not to watch the subsequent performance.

And in response, all creation praises God: "Praise the LORD from the earth, you great sea creatures and all ocean depths . . . wild animals and all cattle, small creatures and flying birds. . . . Let them praise the name of the LORD, for his name alone is exalted; his splendor is above the earth and the heavens" (Ps. 148:7, 10, 13).

The prophets foretold a time when animals and humans would once again live in peace, and Jesus lived out that reality when he was with the wild animals in the wilderness (Mark 1:13).

There is a better way to share the earth with animals than the ways we have inherited and continued. If we are living in and into the anticipation of a world "on earth as it is in heaven," shouldn't we take the simple steps to ensure that animals living in and out of the wild are cared for and protected and no longer need to live in fear of us, their stewards?

Discussion Questions

1. Have you ever gone hunting or killed an animal? What was the experience like for you?
2. Have you ever been to a zoo or circus? Do you recall any observations about the animals and their habitats?
3. What is your experience of animals in the wild? Or of the wild itself?
4. Do you think keeping animals in captivity is in harmony with our role as stewards? What about hunting them for recreation?

CHAPTER 6

Animals Used for Research

Libby, Mango, Clay, and Tulip

In the fall of 2010, PETA rescued nearly 250 dogs and cats from a laboratory run by Professional Laboratory and Research Services, Inc. (PLRS). The lab had been shut down following a PETA undercover investigation that revealed employees kicking, throwing, and dragging dogs, screaming obscenities at animals, and engaging in other abuses. PLRS was contracted by pharmaceutical firms to conduct tests on companion animal products, which meant that the dogs and cats in the lab were infected with worms, fleas, and ticks, and then their abraded skin was rubbed with chemicals to test a product's efficacy.

Libby, a sweet brown and white beagle, was among the animals rescued from that lab. Having spent her entire life in a wire cage, she was too terrified to stand. Her teeth were rotten, she had a vaginal infection, and her emaciated body was infested with hookworms and tapeworms.

The University of Wisconsin–Madison kept Mango in a barren wire cage for years before the lab shut down and he was adopted by a local family. Mango, along with dozens of other cats over decades of research in the same lab, was used for archaic sound-location experiments. Sounds pretty harmless, but what it means is that holes were drilled into Mango's skull, metal restraint posts were screwed into his head, and steel coils were implanted in his eyes.

Clay was born in 1987 at a medical research lab. Taken from his mother ten hours after birth, he was used for the next fifteen years to study ibuprofen, cholesterol medication, and other drugs already approved for use in humans by the Food and Drug Administration (FDA). In 2002 Save the Chimps rescued Clay and dozens of other chimpanzees from "the Dungeon," the series of dank, dark, concrete cells in which they had spent their entire lives. The rescue devoted a decade to introducing the chimpanzees to one another and to life outside a concrete box. Though chimpanzees typically live in large, multigenerational, multifamily groups, years of isolation and abuse have left Clay too traumatized to socialize with other chimpanzees. He continues to live alone.

Tulip narrowly escaped a grim fate at the hands of University of North Carolina–Chapel Hill researchers. Over the course of two investigations, PETA documented mice and rats routinely denied relief from wounds and disease. Improperly trained technicians mutilated animals during procedures, resulting in mice's eyes being gouged out. Rat pups, just eight days old, were doused with ethyl alcohol and their heads were cut off with scissors, recommendations for sedation by ice—the smallest possible mercy—ignored. Rats, who normally would never drink alcohol, were denied food and water until they drank in desperation and ate their own paper bedding in an attempt to ease the resulting pain. Overcrowded cages meant that baby animals were routinely suffocated or trampled to death. The investigator's complaints to lab management went unanswered.

Tens of millions of animals just like Libby, Mango, Clay, and Tulip are used in US laboratories each year to test personal care products, household cleaners, and pharmaceuticals. Animals are used to conduct trauma training exercises for practicing surgeons and the military, and we also use animals for psychological experiments. This chapter will discuss the basics of animal testing and major objections to the practice.

Expectations and Justifications for Vivisection

> Are not five sparrows sold for two pennies? Yet not one of them is forgotten by God.
>
> —*Luke 12:6*

Often, when people think of animal testing, they assume (I know I did) that tests are done only when necessary to discover something new, that animal tests are required by law, that the use of animals in labs is needed in order to help humans, that the minimum amount of pain and suffering is allowed, and that laboratories are clean and sanitary places where the needs of animals are placed on par with the needs of the scientists and their constituents. All of these assumptions are incorrect, a statement on which I will expand in the following section.

But let's pretend, for a moment, that vivisection—experiments on living animals—met some of the above expectations: that animals were kept in comfort, that their suffering was minimal, that they received regular and competent veterinary care, that they were euthanized in a timely and painless manner, and that the results of the tests conducted were the only way to help humans flourish. Even so, would it be right to conduct experiments on living, sentient creatures? Is that why God made animals?

C. S. Lewis wasn't sure. In fact, he called the prevalence of vivisection "a great advance in the triumph of ruthless, non-moral utilitarianism over the old world of ethical law; a triumph in which we, as well as animals, are already the victims."[1] We can see glimpses of his dis-ease with vivisection in *The Magician's*

Nephew. Uncle Andrew is the vivisector who justifies the use of guinea pigs because "that's what the creatures were for. I'd bought them myself."[2] But does might equal right?

Before Narnia, Lewis published an essay through the New England Anti-Vivisection Society called "Vivisection." It is by no means an animal rights treatise, but in it, Lewis points out the contradictory thinking that vivisectors and their supporters often employ to justify the use of animals in their experiments.[3] In his view, "vivisection can only be defended by showing it to be right that one species should suffer in order that another species should be happier."[4] And this, Lewis argues, is where it becomes nearly impossible for a Christian to defend the practice.

Lewis points out that proponents of vivisection frequently defend their acts by claiming that animals have no souls. Of course, we humans do not know this to be fact. More than seventy years after Lewis wrote these words, we now have an even more thorough understanding of the extent to which animals are able to communicate, form relationships and social structures, and display cognition the likes of which Lewis could only imagine in his time. Lewis argues, nevertheless, that without souls, animals are unable to deserve pain or benefit morally from it, and thus the intentional infliction of pain on animals becomes harder, not easier, to justify.

The second line of reasoning provivisectionists may take, according to Lewis, is that humans are superior creatures and their natural place at the top of the food chain gives them a license to use those below them in whatever manner they see fit. As horrific as it sounds today, similar arguments have been made in the past to defend experimentation on humans: Native Americans, Jews, orphans, enslaved persons, destitute African Americans, the deaf, and the physically and mentally delayed. Even if morally significant differences exist between humans and animals (and Lewis believed they did), "we ought to prove

ourselves better than the beasts precisely by the fact of acknowledging duties to them which they do not acknowledge to us."[5]
This is a christocentric view, one in which the powerful forgo
power in order to better serve the powerless.

Faith and science weren't better friends in the 1940s than
they are today, and Lewis acknowledged that most vivisectors
didn't operate under the umbrella of Christian theology. Yet
from a naturalist or Darwinian point of view, Lewis claimed
that the justification for using animals in research stood on even
shakier ground. Lewis saw the danger of such thinking as it took
shape and grew in Nazi Germany: "No argument for experiments on animals can be found which is not also an argument
for experiments on inferior men. If we cut up beasts simply
because they cannot prevent us and because we are backing our
own side in the struggle for existence, it is only logical to cut
up imbeciles, criminals, enemies, or capitalists for the same reasons."[6] Summing up Lewis: I (human) may want to experiment
on you (animal) because you are like me, with flesh and bone
and neurochemical pathways, but because you (animal) are like
me (human), I cannot justify inflicting unnecessary and unde-
served pain on you.

As followers of the One who had mercy on the weak, who
did not inflict wounds but healed them, I do not believe we can
justify the use of animals in experiments. It is to the assumptions
about how animal experiments are conducted and to what end
that we now turn.

Experimentation's Reality

The use of animals in laboratories is regulated in the United
States in three main ways. One is the Animal Welfare Act
(AWA), which is enforced by ninety-six USDA inspectors who
are charged with the oversight of 8,800 institutions. Second,

the Office of Laboratory Animal Welfare enforces the parts of a 1985 act that cover animals used in labs. And finally, voluntary accreditation, available through self-assessment and peer review, is available from the Association for Assessment and Accreditation of Laboratory Animal Care. As a result, some labs are overseen, to various degrees, by three bodies, and others by none.[7] Inspectors are often general veterinarians without specific expertise in laboratory science or the use of animals in labs.[8]

Rats, mice, and birds, the three species who comprise the vast majority of animals used in labs, are not covered under the Animal Welfare Act. According to this legislation,

> *animal* means any live or dead dog, cat, nonhuman primate, guinea pig, hamster, rabbit, or any other warmblooded animal, which is being used, or is intended for use for research, teaching, testing, experimentation, or exhibition purposes, or as a pet. This term excludes birds, rats of the genus *Rattus*, and mice of the genus *Mus*, bred for use in research; horses not used for research purposes; and other farm animals, such as, but not limited to, livestock or poultry used or intended for use as food or fiber, or livestock or poultry used or intended for use for improving animal nutrition, breeding, management, or production efficiency, or for improving the quality of food or fiber. With respect to a dog, the term means all dogs, including those used for hunting, security, or breeding purposes.[9]

In other words, dogs, we'll protect. But chickens and mice are on their own. These limits of protection seem arbitrary at best.

Personal care and household products must be proven safe in order to receive approval from the FDA to go to market. After a consumer outcry in the 1980s, the number of animals used for these types of tests was drastically reduced, but not eliminated.[10] Two primitive yet common testing methods are the Draize and

LD50 (or Lethal Dose 50) tests. The Draize test measures eye irritation by dripping chemicals into the eyes of animals, often rabbits. The LD50 test determines at what dosage half of the animals forced to ingest a chemical will die. The first time I saw an undercover video of a laboratory, it was a brightly lit room full of beagles in wire cages who were in the midst of LD50 testing. Most were very sick, long on their way to death. The investigator filmed as she put her gloved hand in a cage to offer a small measure of comfort to one dog who was foaming at the mouth and too weak to stand. His small body pressed against the back and side of his cage, his eyes pleading for mercy as poison wracked his body.

The laws that govern the use of animals in labs recommend that vivisectors work to minimize pain, unless it's necessary not to, and that if an experiment would cause chronic pain, that the animal in question be euthanized.[11] Vivisectors are charged with ensuring that their experiment doesn't duplicate previous experiments, that alternatives to the use of animals have been considered, and that pain relief or sedatives are used, again unless it is necessary to withhold relief. Regulations even go so far as to require that surgeries be performed in clean, sterile environments and that pre- and postoperative care is provided.

This is the law, but you'll notice the word "necessary." It's up to the vivisectors to determine what's necessary. Violations of the law are rampant, evidenced by twenty years of OIG (Office of the Inspector General) reports highlighting inadequate oversight of institutional animal use committees and failure to adhere to AWA standards.[12] In one Harvard University–run laboratory, a dozen monkeys died of dehydration between 1999 and 2011, a result of "problems with animal care."[13]

In addition, animal tests are often an ineffective and unreliable source of data in the search for cures for human disease.[14] In 1998, the former director of the National Cancer Institute declared,

"The history of cancer research has been a history of curing cancer in the mouse. We have cured mice of cancer for decades—and it simply didn't work in humans."[15] Relying on animal testing is further dangerous for humans in three major ways:[16]

1. Animal testing frequently fails to predict a drug's success in humans. In 2006, the Secretary of Health and Human Services announced that "nine out of ten experimental drugs fail in clinical studies because we cannot accurately predict how they will behave in people based on laboratory and animal studies."[17]

2. Relying on animal testing means that potentially lifesaving drugs are delayed or discarded because of the negative effects in animals, effects that may not appear in humans.

3. Spending time and money on animal tests redirects billions of dollars from tests based on sophisticated and more effective methods.

A number of alternatives to animal testing are available, alternatives that have been validated and/or accepted for use by international regulatory agencies. These methods include *in vitro* cell cultures, computer simulation, and microdosing. Scientists can use blood from human volunteers to test medicines for contaminants; artificial human skin replaces the use of live animals in corrosion and irritation tests; human patient simulators eliminate the use of live animals in trauma training. These methods are proven and available, but animal tests go on.[18]

Despite mountains of evidence that nonanimal methods are safer and more effective than animal methods, and that animal tests are neither necessary nor effective,[19] outdated regulations still require animal tests in some areas (e.g., to test the efficacy of drugs). A landmark study conducted by the National Academy of Sciences criticized animal tests as slow, expensive, and unreliable and called for increased use of nonanimal testing methods.[20] The director of Johns Hopkins University's Center for Alternatives to Animal Testing has criticized the failure of animal testing to predict human outcomes. "There are no such things as sufficiently predictive animal models to substitute for clinical trials. Any drug company would long to have such models for drug development, as the bulk of development costs is incurred in the clinical phase."[21] In other words, by replacing expensive, unreliable, and time-consuming animal tests with nonanimal models of testing, drug companies could develop lifesaving medicine more cheaply (thus making those drugs more accessible for those in financial need).

Animals are often killed during the course of experiments, but occasionally an animal reaches the end of her usefulness and is still alive.[22] What happens then? Most are euthanized. The rest are sold to different labs to endure a new set of experiments.[23] As the use of chimpanzees and other great apes has fallen out of fashion, these highly social and intelligent animals are now warehoused across the nation, though a few fortunate animals are rescued and provided permanent homes in sanctuaries.

Your Tax Dollars at Work

For more than thirty years, Stephen Suomi has been performing maternal deprivation and depression experiments on baby monkeys at his government-funded laboratory in Poolesville, Maryland. Dozens of baby monkeys are born at the lab each year. Many are taken from their mothers within a few hours of birth; some are given a "surrogate" mother—a cloth-covered bottle. It probably comes as no shock to you to learn that infants separated from their mother are miserable.

In one experiment, Suomi straps a mother monkey into a car seat in a cage, sedates her, and covers her nipples. Her baby is put into the cage and experimenters watch as the infant frantically tries to elicit a response from his barely conscious mother. Experimenters may release an electronic snake into the cage to observe the baby's terrified reaction. Some monkeys are shuttled between government-funded labs where they have metal devices screwed into their heads so that researchers can inject drugs already on the market into their brains or intentionally addict them to alcohol.[24]

Neurologist and public health specialist Aysha Akhtar describes a video that she watched an experimenter show to a group of his peers at a neurology conference. He had crushed the spine of a cat, implanted electrodes into her brain, and was forcing her paralyzed body to attempt to walk on a treadmill. She fell off again and again. One time, the experimenter picked her up and she rubbed her head against the palm of his hand. Through her pain and suffering, she was seeking affection.[25]

At the publicly funded US Meat Animal Research Center in Nebraska, the USDA conducts experiments to attempt to increase the already bulging output of factory farms. So-called "easy care" sheep are left to give birth in fields alone. In one weekend, out of twenty-five "ragdoll" baby lambs born, five had been abandoned by their overtaxed mothers, six had respiratory infections, and five had been eaten by wild animals. Pigs bred to be "lean" can't reproduce properly, so females undergo operations on their brains and reproductive organs. In a libido study at the facility, a young cow was mounted repeatedly over hours by half a dozen bulls, her head immobilized to prevent her escape. A vet was called only after her legs had broken beneath her, her body "torn up." The vet recommended immediate euthanasia, but the head scientist, who needed to grant permission, couldn't be found. Hours later, the cow finally succumbed to her injuries.[26]

When we allow ourselves to inflict pain and suffering on animals, we are "objectifying" them—we no longer see them and allow them to exist as subjects of themselves, as beings created by God to glorify and serve God. What happens to humans when they cause suffering, when they knowingly inflict pain, when they are continually violent toward another living creature? We noted earlier the clear link connecting violence to animals with violence to humans. We tend to be able to continue sinful behavior by justifying it to ourselves or by distancing ourselves from those to whom we cause pain. Just as knowing the name of the cow might make it harder to eat the hamburger, "distancing might make it easier to use animals in research in which animals are harmed or killed. Among the devices used in distancing are objectifying animals by referring to them as 'it' and 'which' and using terms as . . . 'culling' to refer to killing."[27]

Consider the care with which God crafted the world and the intimacy God shares with all of creation. Consider that we have been charged to love God and to love one another. Consider the fear endured by the monkeys in Suomi's laboratory. Consider the pain of the cow who was mounted to death at the Meat Animal Research Center in Nebraska. Now consider the pain that horrific act may have caused her Creator. Consider the sorrow experienced by families each year as they watch loved ones die of diseases that human ingenuity might have cured, if not for decades wasted on animal experiments.[28] In our attempts to make the world a little healthier and safer for humans, might we better live into our charge to care for the planet and all its inhabitants by refraining from actions that cause more harm, more suffering, more death?

Discussion Questions

1. How has the justification for testing on animals been presented to you before? What flaws do you see in arguments for and against animal testing?
2. Do you use cruelty-free products (products not tested on animals)? If so, why? If not, why not?
3. Do you believe that nonanimal testing methods should be used whenever possible? Why or why not?

CHAPTER 7

Animals Used for Food and Clothing

Ted and Leo

In 2013, when Farm Sanctuary's Emergency Rescue Team was called to a small dairy farm in New York, team members found two miserable male calves tethered by bailing twine to separate feces- and mud-caked stalls. The tethers were so short the two calves couldn't lie down, and though their stalls were side by side, they had never met one another. Malnourished and grossly underweight, Ted and Leo were rushed to the vet. For seven months, the pair had "lived" like this, tied to a barn wall. The outlines of Leo's bones were visible, and Ted's body was less than half the size it should have been.

Cows produce milk for the same reason that humans do: to feed their babies. Dairy farms impregnate mother cows, then take their calves from them shortly after birth. Female calves are often added to the dairy herd to live the same life of impregnation, birth, and loss. Male calves are frequently tethered into a crate so small they cannot turn around or lie down. Their anemic, undernourished bodies are sold after four months for veal. Others are sold for beef, but their small bodies don't fetch the same price as larger breeds of cow. There's little financial incentive for dairy farms to care for male calves.

When Ted and Leo first arrived at Farm Sanctuary—a farmed-animal sanctuary and nonprofit educational organization in New York—their digestive systems were too damaged to be able to eat grass in any normal quantity. And though their bodies were weak, the first time they stepped into a grassy field and felt sunshine on their backs, they both bucked with joy.[1]

Expectations

The righteous care for the needs of their animals, but the kindest acts of the wicked are cruel.

—*Proverbs 12:10*

When I ate meat, I didn't give much thought to how the animal was raised and killed. Frankly, I didn't give much thought to the fact that I was eating an animal, or I likely would have gone vegan earlier in life. Everything I knew about farming I learned from reading *Little House on the Prairie* and *A Day No Pigs Would Die*. Meat, I thought, came from farmers who had a few animals, cared well for them, and knew them by name. At some point the animals were killed as quickly and reverently as possible by the people who had raised them. It wasn't a job I wanted, but since I thought we had to eat meat to survive, I accepted it and opened my mouth.

Meat and dairy production in today's developed world doesn't look like it did in the Wild West, or even the way it did in the 1920s and '30s, when my grandparents were growing up on their farms. Production methods have changed dramatically over the last century, and as consumer awareness increases, marketing messages have changed too. Many people today feel better eating meat, dairy, and eggs if they know they're from animals who were "free range," "grass fed," or "cage free." Fast casual chain restaurants assure us that the meat they sell comes from "naturally raised" animals as they show us photos of piglets in fields and cows on bright green lawns.[2] But the truth is, these buzzwords carry no legal or moral weight.

We can be similarly misled when it comes to our clothing. I tried on a mothball-smelling vintage mink coat hanging in my best friend's mother's closet once, and it felt way more creepy than glamorous, a feeling that was confirmed when we spied the fox stole tucked even farther back, head and eyes and all. Leather and wool were a different story. I assumed, like many others, that sheep needed to be shorn and that leather was a by-product of the meat industry, that it would be a waste not to wear the skin of the cow I freely ate. I assumed that the animals who gave their wool and skin were treated well. (They had to be, didn't they, or else it would show?)

When I stopped to question my menu or clothing choices, I generally painted the rosiest picture I could and moved on because, after all, there were no alternatives, even if I did sense something could be wrong. And besides, I really liked cheese.

Reality

> "The multitude of your sacrifices—what are they to me?" says the LORD. "I have more than enough of burnt offerings, of rams and the fat of fattened animals; I have no pleasure in the blood of bulls and lambs and goats."
>
> —*Isaiah 1:11*

Eating animal protein is now as bad for humans and the planet as it is for animals. And while being raised and killed for food has probably never been a cakewalk, animals bred and raised in today's system are subjected to abuse long before the killing blade reaches their throats.

The USDA helpfully keeps track of the numbers of animals slaughtered at federally inspected slaughterhouses. Here's who we killed for food in 2014, not including the less-eaten animals like goats, sheep, and rabbits:[3]

- Cows and calves: 30,736,700
- Pigs: 106,878,300
- Chickens and turkeys: 8,889,486,900

Americans also eat a lot of sea animals, but production is measured by weight, not lives. The National Oceanic and Atmospheric Administration (NOAA) tells us that US commercial fishermen caught 9.6 billion pounds of sea animals in 2012, during which year the United States consumed 4.5 billion pounds of both wild-caught and farmed sea animals.[4]

It's hard to imagine what billions of something looks like. But what it means is that every second—every single second—317 animals, not including fish, are being strung up by their legs and having their throats slit in a slaughterhouse. That's in the United States alone.

There are about 319 million people living in the United States today. In 2014, we ate 91 billion pounds of pig, cow, and bird flesh.[5] That's about 288 pounds of meat per person. In 1960 (the first year for which data is available for both meat and poultry), we ate about 177 pounds of meat per person in the United States. Our consumption and demand have increased, so farms have increased their production. The result is that animals are increasingly treated not as creatures in their own right, but as production units. They are product and profit. Communities, the environment, and workers all suffer the consequences of a system born out of commodification.

How Animals Used for Food Live before They Die

The system of raising and killing animals for food is so big it's difficult to know where to start describing it. Here's the short(ish) version.

Mother animals are forcefully impregnated in order to produce litter after litter, baby after baby. These babies are taken from them shortly after birth. Small, sick babies are beaten to death or simply left to die. Pigs and cows who fail to thrive, who do not grow fast enough, meet the same fate. Animals healthy enough to survive are mutilated without painkillers, kept in cramped and filthy conditions, and deprived of every natural instinct until they are big enough and old enough—a few months (chickens) to a couple of years (cows)—to send to slaughter. Mother animals, including cows used for dairy, endure the same living conditions and meet the same fate as their babies when their bodies are no longer able to produce enough babies or milk. Mother and baby bodies alike are often broken and diseased by the time they are killed. At slaughter time, lame animals are dragged on and off transport trucks or are beaten or shocked until they walk on their own. Workers in chicken houses walk through and grab animals by the handful, flinging them into crates. These practices are all standard and legal.

After a long journey in the back of a truck, exposed to all weather extremes, and during which many sick animals die, the animals are dumped at a slaughterhouse. In the winter, pigs sometimes freeze to the sides of trucks and need to be ripped off. Inside the slaughterhouse, animals are hung by their legs in shackles and frequently inadequately stunned before their throats are slit, thus conscious and able to feel pain. Animals may be alive when they are dunked into scalding or defeathering tanks or when workers begin to slice off their limbs. Countless undercover investigations have revealed common practices both on farms and in slaughterhouses that are far worse than the everyday cruelties allowed by law, including beatings, unchecked and untreated disease, mortal injuries, sexual abuse,[6] and more.

One federal law governs the treatment of animals used for food and clothing: the Humane Slaughter Act. It applies *only* to animals at the slaughterhouse and does not govern their birth, lives, or transport. Its enforcement is irregular, and chickens and turkeys, the vast majority of animals killed for food, are exempt from the law. As of this writing, fourteen states have statutes that govern the use of animals for food and clothing.[7] Many of these laws simply state that local jurisdictions cannot create laws more restrictive than what the state or federal laws mandate.

To raise a huge number of animals in a finite space, quarters have to be tight. You may have heard of Confined Animal Feeding Operations (CAFOs) or factory farms. These are now the norm. The vast majority of the animal protein bought and consumed by Americans comes from farms that have a lot of animals in a small space. It's no longer necessary to qualify "factory" farms, and "local" does not mean "humane." Indeed, one of America's most popular exports has been industrialized farming: "Small farms with free-roaming animals are disappearing in many parts of the world. . . . Currently, three-quarters of the world's poultry supply, half of the pork and two-thirds of the eggs come from industrial meat factories."[8]

Farms and slaughterhouses are concentrated in specific areas, and they raise and kill massive numbers of animals. The state of Georgia alone killed 1.2 billion animals in 2013, most of them chickens.[9] The industry claims that CAFOs and routine mutilations—such as debeaking, tail docking, and dehorning—are for the benefit of the animals and the safety of the food supply. Unpack the language, however, and it's not hard to see the reality: to meet the demand for cheap animal protein, animals suffer both in life and in death.

Animal welfare advocates in a few states have attempted to relieve a small measure of farmed-animal suffering by urging the passage of legislation that requires farms to allow pigs, chickens, and cows enough space to turn around and lie down. That bare minimum standard of care is now being legislated because it was not being met by those in agribusiness of their own free will, nor was it demanded by a largely complacent public.

Here is the wording of some of the hardest-fought laws as they relate to pig housing, specifically gestation crates—narrow metal pens in which mother pigs are kept whenever they are pregnant (which is most of the time):

- In Maine: "A person may not tether or confine a covered animal for all or the majority of a day in a manner that prevents the animal from: A. Lying down, standing up and fully extending the animal's limbs; and B. Turning around freely" (7 MRSA §4020).

- In Florida: "It shall be unlawful for any person to confine a pig during pregnancy in an enclosure, or to tether a pig during pregnancy, on a farm in such a way that she is prevented from turning around freely" (Fla. Const. art. 10, §21). The law excludes mention of medical treatment and the prebirthing period and does not define the length of that period.

- In Colorado: "A gestating sow shall be kept in a manner that allows the sow to stand up, lie down, and turn around without touching the sides of its enclosure until no earlier than twelve days prior to the expected date of farrowing. At that time, a gestating sow may be kept in a farrowing unit" (Colo. Rev. Stat. §§35-50.5-101 to 35-50.5-103). This law doesn't go into effect until January 1, 2018, so right now, mother pigs in Colorado are not legally obligated this small measure of care.

Similar laws exist in California, Oregon, Arizona, and Michigan. The National Pork Producers Council (the pork lobby) vigorously opposes gestation crate regulations.[10] Gestation crates are too small for pigs to turn around in or to lie down in comfortably. Crate floors are often slatted or grated, because pigs in gestation crates are forced to sleep, eat, and relieve them-selves in the same tiny area.

There are no minimum required sizes for gestation crates. The American Veterinary Medical Association (AVMA) states that gestation crates are "approximately 6.5 feet long and 2.5 feet wide. . . . Facilities with older installations may include stalls of narrower widths."[11] The AVMA points out that pigs in gestation crates are less active and spend more time sitting and standing and less time walking than pigs housed in pens and that gestation crates prevent pigs from turning around, being with other pigs, or moving to "preferred microenvironments" (i.e., away from their own urine and feces). Pigs in stalls and crates are more likely to be injured and engage in damaging behaviors such as biting, chewing, licking, and rubbing.

In other words, pigs in gestation crates are unhealthy, stressed, and dirty.

According to the AVMA, gestation crates were developed to maximize the use of space and monitor the caloric and nutri-tional intake of mother pigs. As we began to produce more and more pig flesh, old-fashioned family and pasture housing got too crowded. Pigs began fighting with one another for food and babies would frequently die. Instead of producing less pig flesh, modern ingenuity created the gestation crate. The alternative, giving pigs more space, costs more.[12]

Chickens used for meat and eggs are also forced to live in cramped filth. In fact, chickens were the first animals to be raised intensively, and the practice was so profitable that it even-tually spread to include nearly all animals raised for food.

Each adult bird has about the space of a single piece of note-book paper on which to eat, sleep, and relieve themselves. It is not enough space to freely stretch even a single wing. Sick and dying birds are not given veterinary care, and dead birds are fre-quently left in cages with the living. While the AVMA advises that cages be configured in such a way to prevent manure and urine from birds in upper cages falling on those below, this recommendation is frequently ignored. The AVMA acknowledges that smaller cages increase bird deaths but has refused to recommend a minimum size for cages.[13] As with pigs, state laws that cover chickens require a minimum of provision. Michigan's law declares that "notwithstanding any other provision of law, a farm owner or operator shall not tether or confine any covered animal on a farm for all or the majority of any day, in a manner that prevents such animal from doing any of the following: (a) Lying down, standing up, or fully extending its limbs. (b) Turning around freely."[14]

One of the reasons that cages were developed for chickens was to reduce the instance of disease and death from predators. The other was because cages "simplified husbandry by increasing efficiency and requir[ing] less real estate."[15] Cramming chickens into a smaller space costs less and earns producers more money.

Living in cramped and filthy conditions isn't the only suffering experienced by animals raised and killed for food in the United States. Cows, pigs, chickens, and turkeys are subject to routine mutilations without the benefit of painkillers. To prevent pigs from biting one another, for instance, their teeth are pulled out. To prevent chickens from pecking one another, their beaks are cut off. To prevent cows from flicking their tails (spreading mud and manure from their filthy stalls) or goring each other (either on purpose, out of frustration, or by accident), their tails and horns are cut off. To identify a cow as one company's property, burns are inflicted on the flesh. And male cows and pigs are castrated, usually with pliers or rubber bands, while they're babies.

The disbudding and dehorning of cattle in the United States are not currently regulated and are performed largely for financial reasons, since "dehorned cattle require less feeding trough space; are easier and less dangerous to handle and transport; present a lower risk of interference from dominant animals at feeding time; pose a reduced risk of injury to udders, flanks, and eyes of other cattle; present a lower injury risk for handlers, horses, and dogs; exhibit fewer aggressive behaviors associated with individual dominance; and may incur fewer financial penalties on sale."[16] Male and female calves are born with horn buds, and there are several removal methods, all of which cause physical and physiological distress. Buds might be gouged out with a tool that looks like an ice-cream scoop or burned off with caustic chemicals. Horns might be sawed off or cut off with hot wires or pliers. Pain relief, either before, during, or after the mutilation, is rarely provided.

Male calves and piglets are castrated to increase the value of their flesh for meat.[17] No painkillers, either before or after the procedure, are required. And "procedure" is a generous word; in many cases, a farmworker simply picks up the baby pigs, twists off their testicles with pliers, and tosses them back into their stalls.[18]

For identification purposes, pigs and cows are branded or tagged. Recently I spent time with some mother pigs who had been used in a veterinary school breeding program. They had been confined in gestation crates most of their lives, and now their bodies were too sick to produce any more litters. They were on a truck headed to slaughter when PETA intervened, coming to their rescue with funds donated by *The Simpsons* cocreator Sam Simon and convincing the driver to take them to a sanctuary instead. Each pig had a number spray-painted on her back or side, a tag glued to her skin, and four tags punched into an ear, each about one-quarter inch thick. The sanctuary caretaker worked slowly and carefully to remove each of the skin and ear tags, but some of the wounds were so tender that she was unable to offer even this small relief at the risk of causing further injury.

I also recently watched a news program about nuns in Colorado running a cattle farm. They call their work a spiritual discipline, and one of their chores is to restrain calves' heads in a metal grate and burn a mark into their flesh. Both the news program and my experience with the rescued pigs have reminded me how far we have removed ourselves from the embodied reality of being part of the community of creation. Castration, branding, and other mutilations are a pain-filled precursor to a gruesome and pain-filled slaughter. But most of us consume the products of this pain without considering that the source was once a living, breathing, being. Jesus reminds us that our God is the God of flesh and bone and blood and heart. He puts his divine hands on the wounds of the world. The water from his divine mouth mixes with earth to make a paste and restores sight to the blind. A word from his divine lips stops suffering and restores outcasts to their communities. As Christians, can we follow the healer and restorer Jesus with integrity while mutilating our animal neighbors?

Though they are smaller, chickens and turkeys don't escape routine mutilations. When left to their chicken-ness, flocks of chickens will peck one another to establish a hierarchy. On modern farms, this behavior is exacerbated and made dangerous by overcrowding and stressful conditions. Instead of making more room or giving chickens toys and other items to stimulate their minds and stave off boredom, farmers debeak them. It's called "beak trimming" and involves the removal of up to one-third of the upper beak (or the upper and lower beak). Since God made chickens to use their beaks for a variety of important functions requiring sensitivity, it's no surprise that AVMA calls beak trimming "acutely painful"[19] and points out that debeaking causes "difficulty in feeding . . . short-term pain, chronic pain, and acute stress"[20] in birds who undergo the mutilation.

In addition to harmful living conditions and mutilations,

farmers regularly engage in other practices unhealthful for animals in order to boost financial production. For instance, since consumers like breast meat, farmers now breed chickens who grow so top-heavy that their legs can't keep up. Walk into a broiler barn and you'll encounter not only the overwhelming stench of ammonia, dust, and feathers, but also the sight of tens of thousands of birds too crippled to walk. Some birds die of thirst because they are unable to reach water.

Cows used for dairy also pay the price for increased demand. The average milk production of a single dairy cow more than doubled from 1970 to 2007.[21] The average herd size increased, too, from twenty cows to one hundred, while the total number of dairies declined.[22] As a result of being bred and drugged to produce more milk, cows used for dairy suffer from mastitis and painful, debilitating hoof and foot problems, for which veterinary care is frequently delayed or denied.

Pigs aren't exempt. Wild pigs produce an average of five to six pigs per litter, but pigs on farms today give birth to litters of up to fourteen piglets, many of whom die before they are weaned.[23] To reach higher "pigs per litter" rates (with low stillbirths), each pig needs to drink more water than she naturally would, so farmers will sometimes put food into a water bowl so the pig cannot eat without first drinking the water.[24] Pig litters are getting so big that "nurse sows" are now needed to help raise the piglets.[25]

When a dairy cow or laying hen or mother pig is no longer profitable, she's shipped to slaughter along with the billions of other animals whose sole purpose from birth was to be killed for their flesh. The Humane Slaughter Act mandates that livestock (i.e., cows and pigs) are rendered insensible to pain prior to slaughter, but it makes no such demand on the slaughter of chickens, turkeys, or fish.

At slaughter, animals are pushed, prodded, or dumped off of trucks. Chickens are unloaded onto a conveyer belt where workers pick them up and slam their feet into shackles, at a rate of between 140 and 180 birds per minute per line.[26] Upside down, wings flapping, trying to escape, they are run through an electrified stun bath, which is supposed to knock them out long enough for them to reach the automatic killing blade. But the bath doesn't always work and chickens are frequently still struggling as they pass the blade, which often misses their throats and instead slashes their wings or bodies. Backup cutters try to manually slit the throats of still-living birds, but the lines move quickly and more than a million birds each year are still alive when they enter the scalding tanks.

One Louisville slaughterhouse kills 10,500 pigs per day. A fairly typical slaughterhouse, the lines move quickly and workers struggle to keep pace. Equipment, such as the stun wands, may malfunction, and some pigs are shot with a captive bolt gun multiple times before finally dying. After they are stunned, cows and pigs are hoisted upside down by chains. Watch any undercover video and you'll see that many are still kicking, twisting, trying to get free as their throats are slit open and blood begins to pour out.

The Federal Slaughter Inspection Service (FSIS) is charged with conducting inspections at slaughter facilities and verifying that establishments follow food safety and humane handling regulations.[27] It is impossible to inspect all animals due to sheer volume. Each federal inspector is responsible for the impossible task of reviewing "2.33 carcasses per second, 8,400 carcasses per hour, or 67,200 carcasses per eight-hour shift."[28] One study found that when factory employees checked chickens for defects rather than their being checked by a federal inspector, the "average error rate . . . was 64 percent and 87 percent in turkey slaughter facilities."[29]

"Defects" can indicate evidence that an animal wasn't properly stunned before slaughter, or was so mistreated that evidence of abuse is present in their flesh. Inspectors find defects when the killing blade slices into a bird's body instead of her throat, rupturing her intestines and spilling feces into her body cavity. Or they find defects when birds are alive when they enter the boiling water of the defeathering tanks. They find defects when a bird is sick or broken from abuse. The diseases that so often lead to consumer product recalls—and that is all animals can be in this industry: products for consumption—including campylobacter, listeria, and salmonella, are a symptom of the filth and mistreatment rampant in the animal agriculture industry.

Impacts

Sin disrupted the symbiotic harmony of Eden and brought violence into the world. It should come as no surprise that the modern world has developed wholesale systems that subvert the *shalom* of God's creation. Those systems have caused widespread damage, not only to animals, but also to the environment and humans.

Though "creation care" advocates today are quick to ask congregations to ride their bikes to Sunday services or to use recycled paper plates at the annual picnic, it is rarer for an environmental organization to acknowledge the impact that meat-and-dairy-based diets have on the planet. Globally, the raising and killing of animals is responsible for more greenhouse gas emissions than the entire transportation sector—more than all cars, boats, airplanes, and trains.[30] Raising and killing animals for food and clothing, in the manner and scale that we do, harms our environment.

As it turns out, feeding, housing, watering, and dealing with the waste of animals used for food is an astonishingly poor use of resources. Consider how inefficient it is to feed grain and water to animals who will produce a fraction of the caloric value they consume. It takes up to 16 pounds of grain to produce a single pound of meat, and nearly 2,000 gallons of water. Compare that with a protein source like chickpeas, which require 501 gallons of water per pound. Gram for gram, plant-based proteins are more efficient and better for the environment. For each gram of plant-based protein (i.e., beans and lentils), about 5 gallons of water is required. Eggs need 7.7 gallons of water per gram of protein, and chicken requires 9 gallons of water per gram of protein. Beef requires nearly 30 gallons of water per gram of protein.[31] In a world in which billions of people aren't getting enough to eat or drink, the resource drain involved in animal food production ought to trouble us.

In a multicontinent study on the impact of animals used for food, study authors argued that reducing the environmental impact of animals used for food and establishing sustainable levels of animal-protein consumption are "essential for the sustainability of the global food system."[32]

As forests and other ecosystems are converted to pastureland to accommodate animals, the inefficiency of using animals for food increases, particularly in places like sub-Saharan Africa, where one in four people is undernourished and in which a cow may need to consume many times more grass for each gram of protein, because the grasses lack the nutrient density of feeds in other parts of the world.[33] In other words, it can be inefficient to raise cattle in developing nations in part because humans need to eat the good-quality food, leaving animals with foods that are lower in nutritional value.[34]

Imagine what would happen if we in the wealthy global North greatly diminished or even eliminated the use of animals for food. Population trends certainly push in this direction: "By some estimates, global food production would need to double by 2050 if we expect to feed the growing population. The prospect of attaining this goal is severely limited by the amount of agricultural land devoted to raising animals for food. In North America, for example, only 40 percent of cropland is devoted to growing food for direct human consumption; the bulk of the remainder is devoted to feed crops."[35]

Industrial farming is a dirty business. Runoff and odor, the creation of manure, issues that were manageable when farms were small, now cause significant problems,[36] particularly among people who live in communities near to or downstream from farms. "Odors from nearby operations are more than just unpleasant smells; they have been associated with high blood pressure, depression, anxiety, sleep disturbances, and other harms. These and other impacts contribute to the social and economic decline of our nation's rural communities," according to the Johns Hopkins Bloomburg School of Public Health.[37] Feces, urine, and chemicals from farms have been shown to pollute local water supplies and decimate local marine life.[38] Moreover, the chemicals required to tan hides for leather and to treat fur are devastating to local ecosystems and the people who work in these toxic facilities.[39] And when manure spills unexpectedly, as it often does, the consequences are much worse.

Antibiotics and Superbugs

For the first couple of years of his life, my son had ear infections twice a year or so. Nothing so bad as to require surgery or drastic measures, but still very uncomfortable for an infant. It was a blessing that he could get quick relief from antibiotics (and a blessing that we had access to health care that paid for the doctor visit and the drugs). Yet as farms have crammed more and more animals into smaller spaces, disease in farmed animals has skyrocketed. The FDA recently reported that 80 percent of antibiotics sold in the United States are used in farmed animals, the vast majority of those being administered through food and water.[40] How do these two stories connect? Though antibiotic drugs "have been called the health miracle of the last 500 years,"[41] the rampant use of antibiotics in farmed animals is one of the factors leading to the evolution of antibiotic-resistant bacteria responsible for the deaths of one hundred thousand Americans each year.[42]

Impact on Biodiversity

God created a world rich in diversity, where plants and microorganisms and animals and humans could coexist, where working the land could increase all flourishing. As we have increased our production of animal-based products, the land has become stripped of nutrients and soil. Both plant and animal species are disappearing at an increasing rate as forests are razed and replaced with grazing land or monoculture crops.[43] Worldwide, "the natural resources that sustain [livestock] agriculture, such as land and water, are becoming scarcer and are increasingly threatened by degradation and climate change."[44]

Fur, Wool, Down, and Leather

What I've described above, about the life and death of animals used for food and the impact of mass animal farms on the environment, applies to animals whose skins we use as well. The Animal Welfare Act excludes animals used for food and fiber from its protections, and few states have laws to protect fur-bearing animals.[45] Yet similar to the ways animals are used for their flesh, the treatment of animals used for their skins generally elevates profits over principle.

Animals on fur farms are kept in wire cages, where they commonly exhibit signs of zoochosis—abnormal or stereotypical behaviors. Fur farm footage shows foxes, minks, and other animals spinning frantically in their cages, biting themselves, and even eating their own babies. When it's time to die, fur farmers may snap the necks of smaller animals, but one of the most frequently used killing methods is anal electrocution, in which a metal clamp is placed in the animal's mouth and a rod inserted into the anus. An electric shock is delivered, causing the animal to suffer the pain of a heart attack before succumbing to death. Other killing methods include gassing or the injection of chemicals that can cause paralysis but not death, resulting in some animals being skinned while still alive.[46]

It can be hard for people to understand why vegans don't wear wool or down. After all, like eggs and milk, these products can, theoretically, be produced without killing.

Sheep don't need to be sheared. In fact, sheep ranchers have to time shearing carefully so that animals are at a lower risk of dying from exposure after the loss of their God-given coat.[47] Over the years, sheep have been bred to grow more wool than they naturally need. This is a human intervention, a human-created problem that would not exist if we simply left sheep alone. God made sheep and gave them wool. Their wool keeps them warm and, like dogs, they shed excess when it's no longer needed.[48]

Shearing can be a bloody business. Since workers are paid by volume, not by the hour, they are incentivized to work quickly, and the sheep suffer the consequences. When PETA investigated shearing sheds across the United States and Australia, investigators saw workers kicking and punching sheep. Shears, wielded too fast and too hard, ripped gaping wounds in sheep's skin, which workers crudely sewed shut on the spot, without veterinary care or painkillers. In an attempt to control one ewe, a shearer twisted her neck so far around that it snapped and she died. He pushed her back in her pen and moved on to the next sheep. Another man held a sheep's mouth shut with his hand while he punched her in the face again and again.[49]

And down? Geese naturally shed their downy feathers, but

down farmers live-pluck geese—that means workers grab geese, rip out their feathers and down, and put the geese back, only to have the process repeated again and again as their wounds heal and their down returns.

Further Discussion

While the decision is ultimately between you and God, the changes I suggest Christians ought to make are significant. When we have grown up accepting the current state of human-animal relations without interrogating the narrative that tells us animals are ours, the first steps can seem daunting. My initial reaction was to grow defensive, to assume that *my* actions were justified. What follows are some of the questions I wrestled with when I first began to examine my everyday choices related to animals in light of my Christian theological foundation.

I understand that Eden was vegan, but God clearly gave humans permission to eat animals after the flood, and the New Testament contains several verses indicating that all things are clean, it's not what goes in your mouth that defiles you, and it's okay to eat meat. Plus, Jesus ate fish, at the very least. So what gives there?

The underlying question is whether it's a sin to eat meat. I look at sin as disobedience, that which separates us from God. Sin is also both personal and structural. In other words, there are personal acts of disobedience, but there are also sinful systems that perpetuate brokenness and evil.

The modern use and abuse of the created world is a system of deep brokenness and significant sin, and this includes the system that breeds, raises, and kills billions upon billions of sentient, God-created, God-loved creatures each year.

Here's how I've come to think about a few of the passages that often come up when I talk about a biblical basis for a vegan diet.

Genesis 9: The situation here is clearly far from ideal. God's words to Noah are: "The fear and dread of you will fall on all the beasts of the earth, and on all the birds in the sky, on every creature that moves along the ground, and on all the fish in the sea; they are given into your hands. Everything that lives and moves about will be food for you. Just as I gave you the green plants, I now give you everything" (vv. 2–3).

Instead of the *shalom*, the peace and symbiosis of Eden, God describes here a new reality in which animals will fear humans, and in which humans will earn that fear through killing. This is not "good," as in Genesis 1; it simply is the way it is now that humans have rejected God's way. God goes on to say that God's covenant is with all flesh on earth, a promise echoed in Hosea 2:18. Animals are part of the covenant of life with God, and they are among those waiting for redemption from the sin that humans brought into the world.

Acts 10:12–25 and 1 Timothy 4:1–5: Peter's vision, the one in which God told him to "kill and eat," greatly puzzled Peter. He took a few days to sort it out and eventually realized that what God was telling him through this vision was that the good news is for *all*, not just the Jews, and that he was called to fellowship with and preach the gospel to Gentiles, even to Roman soldiers. The 1 Timothy passage refers to a particular teaching perhaps making the rounds among early Christians that elevated asceticism and made it into a kind of idol. I do not argue in favor of a vegan lifestyle out of idolatry. I don't refuse to eat with meat eaters (and I hope no other vegan Christian does, either) or believe that killing animals for food is any worse than greed, laziness, pride, gossip, or any number of the sins I struggle with every day. Jesus said we are to love God and love others. Being vegan is the best way I know how to love the "others" of creation, both human and non.

I don't know why Jesus ate fish (some scholars argue that he didn't, but the majority do not), but I do know two things. First, the cultural and structural reality of meat-eating two thousand years ago was wildly different than that reality now. Second, Jesus led a radically inclusive life—befriending the rejects, the outcasts . . . the *most* marginalized. It seems to me that many of us today (including me, including now) have failed to follow that clear example. We often ensconce ourselves in bubbles of homogeneity and like-us-ness. Our treatment of animals betrays this bias. We may compartmentalize our service and compassion based on species or perceived utility. It's why so many of us will eat KFC while crying over *Bambi* with our AKC-registered Labraschnoodle resting peacefully by our side.

What we fail to see is that dogs, cats, pigs, and chickens *all* give us the opportunity for love and service, and we don't need to sacrifice our humanness to honor their chicken-ness, pig-ness, cat-ness, or dog-ness. "We are who we are not because we are separate from the others who are next to us, but because we are *both* separate *and* connected, *both* distinct *and* related; the boundaries that mark our identities are both barriers and bridges."[50] In this way, our relationship with God's animals and with one another reflects the Trinitarian nature of God in the world. We are unique and related, mutually interdependent, and our true flourishing depends on the true flourishing of one another. Adopting a vegan diet and lifestyle is one of the easiest ways I have found to honor the gift of God's creation and to follow the example of Jesus' love for all.

If we can do it well, is it okay to use wool, eat eggs, and the like? After all, God clothed Adam and Eve in skins!

I have a friend who has chickens in her back yard, rescued from various situations. It's a small flock, and they each have a name. My friend protects them, provides veterinary care, and makes an effort to ensure that they are happy and have plenty to keep them occupied. When "her girls" get old, they die of natural causes, or if they are in pain, my friend has a veterinarian come to euthanize them. They lay eggs, because that's what chickens do, and I don't mind eating those. They taste delicious, and no one died or suffered to get them to my plate. Instead of focusing on a list of dos and don'ts, on creating a legalistic system in which we make choices out of fear or to toe a party line, I prefer this simple guide: reduce suffering where you can. Nonwool sweaters and mittens will keep you just as warm, so choose them instead of the ones for which an ewe may have suffered or died. Ask for the cheese to be left off of your dinner salad and enjoy the bounty and flavors of the many delicious and healthy plants God created to nourish our bodies. And on and on. Taking the first step is the hardest part.

Don't people need jobs? Won't not farming animals mean a lot of people will lose their livelihood?

In her diaries, Dorothy Day, champion of the poor and powerless, remarks on a day that included the slaughter of a pig. She makes no further comments on the life or death of the pig, indicating a lack of moral concern, question, or dialogue about the implications of the death. "[Dorothy] Day is a telling example of how many people, including those who pride themselves on being 'progressive' (a not-unambiguous term) or 'humanitarian,' have yet to see the killing and suffering of animals as a moral issue. Even for many today, killing is just that: a fact of life, just what it means to live, part of the air we breathe. But it is worth reminding ourselves how much of what we take for granted is socially conditioned and, unless we strive assiduously to think and feel for ourselves, how we are simply slaves to our time."[51] One of the arguments used to justify keeping the institution of slavery intact was the threat of the negative impact of freedom for all. If we move away from using animals for greedy and evil purposes, our economies will adapt. The possibilities are endless, because God created a world of diverse harmony!

Discussion Questions

1. Have you ever thought before about what happens to animals before they end up on our plates? What was your thought process?
2. Would you be willing and/or able to kill an animal to eat him or her? Why or why not?
3. If you are vegetarian or vegan now, why did you stop eating animals?
4. If you are not vegetarian or vegan now, why not?

Conclusion

What's Next?

Until I was a young adult and began looking for information on the use and treatment of animals, I wasn't aware of the extent to which humans had so degraded our relationship with God, creation, and animals. Looking back, I can see there were a few reasons for my ignorance:

1. I had no cause for concern. Not because I thought about whether or not animals were treated humanely, but because it didn't occur to me that they were being misused in any way. They were ghosts. Animal pain and parts fueled my day-to-day reality, but I failed to connect my choices with (once) living, breathing creatures.

2. It had never occurred to me that there was any reason not to eat animals or wear their skins. Only a very few of my weirdest friends with strange hippie parents were vegetarian, and I found it confusing. When a friend of mine went vegan in high school, I belittled him without mercy.

3. Industries that use animals are heavily invested in hiding the harsh realities and ensuring that we don't dig too deep. Consider ag-gag laws, which criminalize undercover investigations—not the acts of cruelty, but the work to expose those acts. Consider how removed farms and slaughterhouses are from major population

centers. Go knock on the door of a Tyson or Hormel slaughterhouse and ask for a tour—let me know how that goes. Ask to observe one of the NIH's tests on baby monkeys. See how far you get, how much industries whose bread is buttered by animal bodies want to show you.

Once I started to understand the disturbing reality of using animals for food, clothing, and experiments, I didn't change right away. It took years for the truth to sink in, for my heart to soften to what I believe God had been trying to show me for a long time.

I've talked to many friends and family members over the years about animal protection issues. No one is happy to hear how animals are mistreated, and only a very few people are unmoved. But once the enormity of the problem sets in, once you realize how much of your life is built on suffering, it can seem a pretty daunting evil to try to overcome. How can one person stem such a tide of misery and violence?

Yet cruelty to animals is one of the few of this fallen world's hideous realities that is actually possible for everyday people to change. I can do little more than offer fervent prayers and donations to organizations doing good work to stop child sex trafficking or to rebuild after a massive earthquake or devastating flood. Choosing not to harm animals is one of the easiest choices I can make every day, and it doesn't require that I become a full-time animal rights activist or forget about other causes that are important to me. Just this week, I participated in a moving and convicting event discussing racial reconciliation and justice, and I ate vegan meals while I was there. When many people make compassionate choices, big changes can happen.

One person who is vegetarian spares more than one hundred animals from a nightmarish life and death every year. When we vote with our dollars, when we refuse to buy products that have been tested on animals, when we choose vegan clothing and food, for us it's just making one choice over another. Yet those choices mean life or death for animals, and the ripple effect is wide. Our choices affect not only our own lives and the lives of animals, but also the lives of people directly impacted by the filth and cruelty of animal-abusing industries and the lives of people in the global South who are disproportionately affected by climate change, of which animal agriculture is a driving factor.

So do you want to make a difference for animals? Just remember these two words: choose kindness. Veggie or beef burger? Leather shoes or man-made materials? Cruelty-free shampoo or the kind that was tested on animals?

When I went vegan, I had to stop my routine of McDonald's every morning, a deli sandwich every lunch, and a meat-centered dinner. I made new routines, walked down different aisles of the grocery store, ordered different entrees at restaurants. Logistically, it wasn't that hard.

Mentally, the transition to a vegan life was harder than I anticipated. I had strong cravings for meat and cheese for a long time, not because my body needed the nutrients—my cholesterol dropped more than seventy points and my blood work was great—but because I was addicted to animal fat. None of my coworkers were vegan, and only one of my friends was. The first time I turned down my grandmother's bone-in ham dinner, she was gracious, but I felt guilty.

Choose kindness. Reduce suffering where you can.

Many excellent resources are available online, on your smartphone, and in good old-fashioned books that can help broaden your awareness of the compassionate choices likely available to you. And don't let anyone tell you that it's expensive to be vegan. Cooking fresh and healthy vegan meals may require a bit of planning (and overnight bean soaking), but expensive it is not. My family could easily reduce our already less-than-average weekly grocery spend by purchasing fewer packaged foods (my son loves Larabars; I really like Tofurky deli slices). We spend five dollars a month on a menu-planning service that ensures we cut down on food waste and eat well-balanced meals (because I'd honestly be okay alternating between Gardein burgers [*Gardein. com*]—seriously, they're the best veggie burger on the market, so savory and delicious—and spaghetti every night, but I think my body and family would eventually rebel).

When I first went vegan, I bought two vegan cookbooks and picked a couple of recipes that looked promising. Vegan cookbooks are jam-packed with information about pantry staples and substitutes. This is where I learned that you can use applesauce instead of eggs in baking and the difference between tofu, tempeh, and seitan.

It took a little over a year to transform my closet. I didn't realize until about four months into my cruelty-free choices that I had dropped a load of pounds and my pants were falling off. So that made replacing the wool easy. I waited until my leather shoes and pocketbook wore out, then replaced them with cute and eco-friendly vegan styles.

By the time my son was born, I'd been choosing vegan for many years. I read up on vegan nutrition during pregnancy and talked to my midwife, but it was pretty much your run-of-the-mill roller-coaster ride. My athletic boy has never had a glass of milk or a bite of meat. He loves to eat beans and tofu when it's cooked just so. He'll pound down salad and thick green smoothies like they're going out of style. His favorite bedtime snack is almonds. Don't get me wrong. His favorite *food* is ice cream, dairy free of course, and he doesn't really like to try new foods. In other words, he's a fairly typical six-year-old.

Choosing cruelty-free personal care and cleaning products is easy now. To save money, we make our own laundry detergent and hand soap, but you can buy cruelty-free brands at grocery stores, health-food co-ops, and Targets all over the country.

Feeling the need to add a furry friend to your pack? Visit a shelter or rescue. Nostalgic for a specific breed? Look up breed-specific rescues and adopt from them. Spay or neuter your new family member to prolong their life, ensure you don't accidentally add to the overpopulation crisis, and help with temperament and behavior issues.

Looking for a vacation spot or a place to spend a sunny Saturday afternoon? Skip the zoos and choose children's museums, botanical gardens, the beach, a mountain hike, a neighborhood bike ride, or any number of healthy activities that leave animals alone. Know where your nearest wildlife rehabilitation center is and take injured animals there with your kids so they can see you and others caring for animals in need.

The Spirit of God is drawing us toward God. Will we resist God's pull and cling to a hope handed to us by the world, one that tells us that might makes right? The Spirit of God is drawing *all* of us together, working in and through the whole creation in a movement toward reconciliation. Will we let ourselves be caught up in the stream of the Spirit?

You and I will make mistakes. We will not be perfect. Such is the nature of our fallen world. But I hope you will join me in praying for and moving toward a world that reflects Jesus' prayer for us, "so that the love with which you have loved me may be in them, and I in them" (John 17:26 NRSV). Perhaps then we not only will see ourselves as the protective mother hen, guarding the vulnerable animals who are calling for our care, but also will act as loving protectors toward all of God's creation.

Notes

Part 1: Theological Foundation

1. Sider's methodology is outlined in many of his books. For this overview, I used the version in Ronald J. Sider, *The Scandal of Evangelical Politics* (Grand Rapids: Baker, 2008).
2. Ibid., 41.

Chapter 1: Made in the Image of the Trinitarian God

1. Jürgen Moltmann, *The Trinity and the Kingdom* (Minneapolis: Augsburg Fortress, 1993), 112.
2. Cynthia Moe-Lobeda, "Climate Change as Climate Debt: Forging a Just Future" (presentation, annual meeting of the Society of Christian Ethics, January 2015).
3. The word translated as "mercy" in the NIV is a beautiful word, *hesed*, which also can mean "covenant loyalty." No English word quite captures the meaning of *hesed*. It is a type of mercy that pushes one on to God, an absolute love.
4. The historical information in this section is gleaned from William C. Placher, "The Trinity," in *Essentials of Christian Theology*, ed. William C. Placher (Louisville: Westminster John Knox, 2003), 56–59.
5. Ibid., 59.
6. Moltmann, *Trinity and Kingdom*, 174–75.
7. Ibid., 176.
8. Domination and oppression aren't the same as judgment and discipline. The former are acts of self-interest motivated by sin. The latter are acts of others-interest motivated by love.
9. Eugene H. Merrill, "Image of God," in *Dictionary of the Old*

Testament Pentateuch, ed. T. Desmond Alexander and David W. Baker (Downers Grove, IL: InterVarsity Press, 2003), 443.

10. J. Richard Middleton, *The Liberating Image: The* Imago Dei *in Genesis 1* (Grand Rapids: Brazos, 2005), 88.

11. Ibid., 90.

12. Randy Woodley, *Shalom and the Community of Creation: An Indigenous Vision* (Grand Rapids: Eerdmans, 2012), 39.

13. Daniel L. Migliore, *Faith Seeking Understanding: An Introduction to Christian Theology* (Grand Rapids: Eerdmans, 2004), 72.

14. Moltmann, *Trinity and Kingdom*, 113.

15. Middleton, *Liberating Image*, 18–19.

16. Murray D. Gow, "Fall," in Alexander and Baker, *Dictionary of Old Testament Pentateuch*, 291.

17. Richard Stearns, "Slaughterhouse Gospel," *Christianity Today*, April 1, 2015, *www.christianitytoday.com/ct/2015/april-web-only/slaughterhouse-gospel-sacrifice.html*.

Chapter 2: Dominion and Stewardship

1. Ellen F. Davis, *Scripture, Culture, and Agriculture: An Agrarian Reading of the Bible* (New York: Cambridge University Press, 2009), 124.

2. "Demographics," *EPA.gov*, last updated April 14, 2013, *www.epa.gov/agriculture/ag101/demographics.html*.

3. Davis, *Scripture, Culture, and Agriculture*, 140.

4. Fred Davies, quoted in Texas A&M AgriLife Communications, "Food Shortages Could Be Most Critical World Issue by Mid-Century." *ScienceDaily: www.sciencedaily.com/releases/2014/04/140417124704.htm* (February 17, 2015).

5. António Guterres, quoted in Leslie Baehr and Chelsey Harvey, "25 Devastating Effects of Climate Change," *Business Insider: www.businessinsider.com/terrible-effects-of-climate-change-2014-10* (February 17, 2015).

6. Ibid., referencing Dieter Gerten et al., "Asynchronous Exposure to Global Warming: Freshwater Resources and Terrestrial Ecosystems," *Environmental Research Letters* 8, no. 3 (September 12, 2013).

7. J. Walsh et al., "Our Changing Climate," chapter 2 in *Climate Change Impacts in the United States: The Third National Climate Assessment*, ed. J. M. Melillo, T. C. Richmond, and G. W. Yohe

(2004), 19–67. *http://nca2014.globalchange.gov/report/our-changing -climate/changes-hurricanes.*

8. Office for Climate Change and Disaster Risk Reduction, "Hunger and Climate Change," *World Food Programme* (November 2010), *http://documents.wfp.org/stellent/groups/public/documents/communications/ wfp227909.pdf.*

9. "Timeline of Extinctions," *Wikipedia*: *http://en.wikipedia.org/wiki/ Timeline_of_extinctions* (February 17, 2015).

10. "Species Extinction—The Facts," *International Union for the Conservation of Nature*: *http://cmsdata.iucn.org/downloads/species_ extinction_05_2007.pdf* (February 21, 2015).

11. "International Decade for Action: 'Water for Life' 2005–2015," *United Nations Department of Economic and Social Affairs*: *www.un.org/ waterforlifedecade/quality.shtml* (February 17, 2015).

12. Environmental Protection Agency, "Air Quality Trends," *EPA.gov*: *www.epa.gov/airtrends/aqtrends.html* (February 17, 2015).

13. "The Extinction Crisis," *Center for Biological Diversity*: *www.biological diversity.org/programs/biodiversity/elements_of_biodiversity/extinction_crisis/* (February 17, 2015).

14. Earth Talk, "Dirt Poor: Have Fruits and Vegetables Become Less Nutritious?" *Scientific American*, April 27, 2011, *www.scientificamerican .com/article/soil-depletion-and-nutrition-loss/.*

15. Davis, *Scripture, Culture, and Agriculture*, 67.

16. Richard Bauckham, *Living with Other Creatures: Green Exegesis and Theology* (Waco, TX: Baylor University Press, 2011), 19.

17. C. S. Lewis, *The Magician's Nephew* (New York: HarperCollins, 1955), 128.

18. Ibid., 151–52.

19. Davis, *Scripture, Culture, and Agriculture*, 164–65.

20. Lewis, *Magician's Nephew*, 190.

21. James McKeown, "Blessings and Curses," in Alexander and Baker, *Dictionary of Old Testament Pentateuch*, 86.

22. Davis, *Scripture, Culture, and Agriculture*, 54–55.

23. Ibid., 55 (emphasis mine).

24. Ibid., 58.

25. Bauckham, *Living with Other Creatures*, 14.

26. Ibid., 5.

27. Ibid., 40.

28. Davis, *Scripture, Culture, and Agriculture*, 54.

29. Bauckham, *Living with Other Creatures*, 227.

30. It even sounds a little violent. Kabash! Like *kapow!* or some other word to denote 1960s Batman stage-punching an evil villain just before he saves the girl.

31. Sarah Withrow King, *Animals Are Not Ours (No, Really, They're Not)* (Eugene, OR: Cascade Books, 2015), 102–3.

32. Davis, *Scripture, Culture, and Agriculture*, 60.

33. Ibid., 64.

34. Bauckham, *Living with Other Creatures*, 86.

35. Ibid., 152.

36. Ibid., 25.

37. Davis, *Scripture, Culture, and Agriculture*, 19–20.

38. Moltmann, *Trinity and Kingdom*, 112.

39. Ibid., 114.

40. Ibid., 214.

41. Ibid., 58.

42. Davis, *Scripture, Culture, and Agriculture*, 64–65.

43. A friend who runs a sanctuary took in dozens of cows from a dairy that tried to be bloodless—male calves weren't sold for their flesh and female cows were not sold to slaughter when they stopped producing milk. The farm went broke. Commercial, bloodless dairy isn't possible.

Chapter 3: Loving the Other

1. Mary J. Evans, "Women," *Dictionary of the Old Testament Historical Books*, ed. Bill T. Arnold and H. G. M. Williamson (Downers Grove, IL: InterVarsity Press, 2005), 990.

2. Miroslav Volf, *Exclusion and Embrace* (Nashville: Abingdon, 1996), 78.

3. Ronald J. Sider, *Just Generosity: A New Vision for Overcoming Poverty in America*, 2nd ed. (Grand Rapids: Baker, 2007), 122.

4. Volf, *Exclusion and Embrace*, 80.

5. Ibid., 75. The following expansions draw on Volf's writing.

6. Ibid., 100.

7. Ibid., 65.

8. Fred Bahnson and Norman Wirzba, *Making Peace with the Land: God's Call to Reconcile with Creation* (Downers Grove, IL: InterVarsity

Press, 2012), 157. While Bahnson and Wirzba's book is inspiring, I often felt while reading it that the authors had more care and concern for trees, microorganisms, and dirt than for flesh-and-blood animals. A frustrating and persistent inconsistency in much "creation care" literature.

9. Volf, *Exclusion and Embrace*, 129.

10. An excellent analysis of Jesus' teachings about the kingdom of God as they relate to the created world can be found in Richard Bauckham, *Living with Other Creatures: Green Exegesis and Theology* (Waco, TX: Baylor University Press, 2011), 70–75.

11. Bahnson and Wirzba, *Making Peace*, 123.

12. Ibid.

13. Bauckham, *Living with Other Creatures*, 108–9.

14. Ibid., 117.

15. Ibid., 110.

16. Bahnson and Wirzba, *Making Peace*, 159. The authors do not make this call to stop eating animals. In fact, they repeatedly glorify those who unnecessarily incorporate the breeding and killing of animals into otherwise sustainable and commendable earth-keeping projects. It is a point of glaring hypocrisy in an otherwise compelling work.

17. Desmond Tutu, *No Future without Forgiveness* (New York: Image Doubleday, 1999).

18. Volf, *Exclusion and Embrace*, 51.

19. Ibid., 88.

Chapter 4: Animals in Our Homes

1. Animal Care and Control Team of Philadelphia, "2015 Shelter Statistics—All Animals," *ACCTPhilly.org*: www.acctphilly.org/wp-content/uploads/2011/01/2015-03-AnimalCare.pdf?936bb7 (May 27, 2015).

2. "A Closer Look at Puppy Mills," *ASPCA*: www.aspca.org/animal-cruelty/puppy-mills/closer-look-puppy-mills (November 16, 2015).

3. Ibid.

4. Ibid.

5. "Pet Statistics," *ASPCA*: www.aspca.org/animal-homelessness/shelter-intake-and-surrender/pet-statistics (November 16, 2015).

6. Norma Bennett Woolf, "Are There Too Many Dogs and Cats?" *National Animal Interest Alliance*, March 19, 1997, *www.naiaonline.org/naia-library/articles/are-there-too-many-dogs-and-cats/*.

7. Oxford-Lafayette Humane Society, "Animal Overpopulation," *OxfordPets.com*: *www.oxfordpets.com/index.php?option=com_content&view=article&id=61* (May 27, 2015).

8. Christopher Matthews, "The World Only Needs 30 Billion Dollars a Year to Eradicate the Scourge of Hunger," *Food and Agriculture Organization of the United Nations*, June 3, 2008, *www.fao.org/news room/en/news/2008/1000853/index.html*.

9. "Cruelty Laws," *StrayPetAdvocacy.org*: *www.straypetadvocacy.org/cruelty_laws.html* (May 27, 2015).

10. Melissa Cronin, "All 50 US States Now Have Felony Charge for Animal Cruelty," *The Dodo*, last updated March 14, 2014, *www.the dodo.com/all-50-us-states-now-have-felo-465803412.html*.

11. Linda Merz-Perez et al., "Childhood Cruelty to Animals and Subsequent Violence against Humans," *International Journal of Offender Therapy and Comparative Criminology* 45, no. 5 (October 2001): 556–73; doi: 10.1177/0306624X01455003.

12. Jeniimarie Febres et al., "Adulthood Animal Abuse among Men Arrested for Domestic Violence," *Violence against Women* 20, no. 9 (September 2014): 1059–77; doi: 10.1177/1077801214549641.

13. Christopher Hensley et al., "Recurrent Childhood Animal Cruelty: Is There a Relationship to Adult Recurrent Interpersonal Violence?" *Criminal Justice Review* 34, no. 2 (June 2009): 248–57; doi: 10.1177/0734016808325062.

14. Bill C. Henry and Cheryl E. Sanders, "Bullying and Animal Abuse: Is There a Connection?" *Society and Animals* 15, no. 2 (2007): 107–26; doi: 10.1163/156853007X187081.

Chapter 5: Animals in (and out of) the Wild

1. "Total Number of Extinct Species: 905 (Was 784 in 2006)," *Endangered Species International*: *www.endangeredspeciesinternational.org/overview1.html* (February 17, 2015).

2. "The Five Worst Mass Extinctions," *Endangered Species International*: *www.endangeredspeciesinternational.org/overview.html* (February 17, 2015).

3. Ibid.

4. "The *Blackfish* Effect: Will It Spark Change?" *Huffington Post*, video, 15:56, January 20, 2014, *http://live.huffingtonpost.com/r/segment/ the-blackfish-effect-will-it-spark-change/52cc10a478c90a6b7900002d*.

5. "Animal Care FAQ," *Ringling Brothers*: *www.ringling.com/ContentPage .aspx?id=45761&section=45696* (May 27, 2015).

6. Deborah Nelson, "The Cruelest Show on Earth," *Mother Jones*, November/December 2011, *www.motherjones.com/environment/2011/ 10/ringling-bros-elephant-abuse* (February 17, 2015).

7. Ibid.

8. Ibid.

9. "USDA Fines Ringling Brothers," *Wildlife Advocacy Project*, November 2011, *www.wildlifeadvocacy.org/current/circus/usda_fines_ ringling.php*.

10. Nelson, "Cruelest Show on Earth."

11. Ibid.

12. Animal rights groups compile and track records of animal care failures at circuses and other places that use animals for entertainment. One example is available here: "Kelly Miller Circus," *People for the Ethical Treatment of Animals*: *www.mediapeta .com/peta/pdf/Kelly-Miller-pdf.pdf* (May 27, 2015).

13. Gabriela Cowperthwaite and Manuel Oteyza, *Blackfish* (New York City: Magnolia Pictures, 2013), DVD.

14. "Killer Whale (Orcinus Orca)," *National Oceanic and Atmospheric Administration Fisheries*, last updated May 14, 2015, *www.nmfs.noaa .gov/pr/species/mammals/whales/killer-whale.html*.

15. Erich Hoyt, *The Performing Orca: Why the Show Must Stop* (Bath, UK: Whale and Dolphin Conservation Society, 1992), chap. 3; published online at *Frontline*: *www.pbs.org/wgbh/pages/frontline/shows/ whales/keiko/world.html* (May 27, 2015).

16. Jared Goodman, quoted in EcoWatch, "Shocking Court Documents Expose SeaWorld's Continued Cruelty of Orca Whales," *EcoWatch. com*: *http://ecowatch.com/2014/04/02/seaworlds-cruelty-orca-whales/* (April 2, 2014).

17. Well, some zoos were. Some zoos started as little sanctuaries for orphaned and injured wildlife, which is lovely. But then they became ways to make money.

18. "Captive Breeding—WWF Policy Statement 2007," *World Wide*

Fund for Nature, last updated May 29, 2007, *http://wwf.panda.org/ ?103860/Captive-Breeding-WWF-Policy-Statement-2007.*

19. For a really good theological reflection on zoos, and one that softened my view of zoos and their role in animal stewardship, read Tripp York's *The End of Captivity* (Eugene, OR: Wipf and Stock, 2015).

20. Sally Jewel et al., "2011 National Survey of Fishing, Hunting, and Wildlife-Associated Recreation," *US Department of the Interior*: *www .census.gov/prod/2012pubs/fhw11-nat.pdf* (May 27, 2015).

21. Maryland Department of Natural Resources, "Deer Hunting: An Effective Management Tool," *Maryland.gov*: *http://dnr2.maryland.gov/ wildlife/Pages/hunt_trap/deerhuntastool.aspx* (May 27, 2015).

22. Google "trophy fee" and an animal and you can find numerous examples of hunt packages and see photos of people posing with animals they paid a lot of money to kill. These figures came from *AfricaHuntLodge.com*.

23. "Red Sheep Hunt," *Texas Hunt Lodge*: *www.texashuntlodge.com/ red_sheep_hunt_package.asp* (May 27, 2015).

24. Katie Rogers, "American Hunter Killed Cecil, Beloved Lion Who Was Lured out of His Sanctuary" *New York Times*, http:// www.nytimes.com/2015/07/29/world/africa/american-hunter-is -accused-of-killing-cecil-a-beloved-lion-in-zimbabwe.html?_r=0 (December 15, 2015).

25. Dave Roos, "Does Deer Hunting Reduce Car Accidents?" *How Stuff Works*: *http://adventure.howstuffworks.com/outdoor-activities/ hunting/principles/deer-hunting-car-accidents1.htm* (May 27, 2015).

26. "Hunting Has Increased Deer Population, Not Reduced It," *Greenwich Time*, September 2, 2010, *www.greenwichtime.com/local/ article/Hunting-has-increased-deer-population-not-643259.php*.

27. I offer this source with a caveat: you can't believe everything you read on the internet. But the author here has catalogued the practices of several states and provides links to official government documents, so she passes: Doris Lyn, "How Are Deer Managed by State Wildlife Agencies?" *http://animalrights.about.com/od/wildlife/a/ DeerManagement.htm*.

28. Eric Bolen and William Robinson, *Wildlife Ecology and Management* (San Francisco: Pearson Benjamin Cummings, 2003), 184.

Chapter 6: Animals Used for Research

1. C. S. Lewis, "Vivisection," *God in the Dock: Essays on Theology and Ethics*, ed. Walter Hooper (Grand Rapids: Eerdmans, 1970), 249.

2. C. S. Lewis, *The Magician's Nephew* (New York: HarperCollins, 1955), 24.

3. Lewis, "Vivisection," 244–49.

4. Ibid., 245.

5. Ibid., 246–47.

6. Ibid., 248.

7. "Comparison to Other Regulatory Services," *Select Committee on Animals in Scientific Procedures Report* (UK Parliament, 2002), 1.14, *www.publications.parliament.uk/pa/ld200102/ldselect/ldanimal/150/15004.htm#a7* (May 27, 2015).

8. Ibid.

9. US Department of Agriculture, *Animal Welfare Act and Animal Welfare Regulations* (Washington, DC: Department of the Interior, 2013), *www.aphis.usda.gov/animal_welfare/downloads/Animal%20Care%20Blue%20Book%20-%202013%20-%20FINAL.pdf*. Emphasis mine.

10. National Research Council of The National Academies, *Science, Medicine, and Animals* (Washington, DC: The National Academics, 2004), *www.nap.edu/read/10733/chapter/1*.

11. Subchapter A—Animal Welfare, *Code of Federal Regulations*, title 9 (2013): § 2.31—Institutional Animal Care and Use Committee, *www.gpo.gov/fdsys/pkg/CFR-2013-title9-vol1/xml/CFR-2013-title9-vol1-chapI-subchapA.xml#seqnum2.129*.

12. See, for example from Office of Inspector General, US Department of Agriculture: "APHIS Animal Care Program, Inspection and Enforcement Activities," audit report, September 30, 2005, and "Animal and Plant Health Inspection Service Oversight of Research Facilities," audit report, December 2014; see also Animal and Plant Health Inspection Service, US Department of Agriculture, "USDA Employee Survey on the Effectiveness of IACUC Regulations," April 2000.

13. Carolyn Y. Johnson, "More Suspicious Monkey Deaths Uncovered at Primate Center," *Boston Globe*, April 8, 2015, *www.bostonglobe.com/metro/2015/04/07/primate/Rn1QvlFUqFH9m4LfU71IrJ/story.html*.

14. Daniel G. Hackam and Donald A. Redelmeier, "Translation of Research Evidence from Animals to Human," *Journal of the American Medical Association* 296 (2006): 1731–32.

15. Marlene Cimons et al., "Cancer-Cure Story Raises New Questions—*New York Times* Reporter Backs Out of Book Deal on New Therapy," *Seattle Times*, May 8, 1998, *http://community .seattletimes.nwsource.com/archive/?date=19980506&slug=2749152*.

16. Aysha Akhtar, "The Top 3 Ways Animal Experiments Hurt Humans," *Huffington Post*, November 11, 2013, *www.huffingtonpost .com/aysha-akhtar/animal-experiments_b_4209541.html*.

17. "FDA Issues Advice to Make Earliest Stages of Clinical Drug Development More Efficient," *US Food and Drug Administration*, January 12, 2006, *www.fda.gov/NewsEvents/Newsroom/ PressAnnouncements/2006/ucm108576.htm*. The consequences of failed tests are devastating. Many drugs that have been deemed safe through animal tests have caused dangerous and deadly side effects in humans, and the reverse is true as well: lifesaving drugs have been delayed because of their adverse effects on animals, including fluoride, Lasix, and insulin.

18. "Frequently Asked Questions: Science," *National Anti-Vivisection Society*: *www.navs.org/about/science-faq* (July 17, 2015).

19. In 2014 the *British Medical Journal* published a paper written by researchers from the University of Bristol and Yale University. The team searched for evidence in support of claims that animal tests benefited humans. Instead, they found many studies that showed animal tests failing to do just that (P. Pound et al., "Where Is the Evidence That Animal Research Benefits Humans? *British Medical Journal* 328 [7438]: 514–17.) This paper followed a 2013 NIH report claiming that "research involving chimpanzees has rarely accelerated new discoveries or the advancement of human health for infectious diseases." You can read the full NIH report here: *https://dpcpsi.nih .gov/sites/default/files/FNL_Report_WG_Chimpanzees_0.pdf*.

20. "Report Calls for New Directions, Innovative Approaches in Testing Chemicals for Toxicity to Humans," *National Academy of Sciences*, June 12, 2007, *www8.nationalacademies.org/onpinews/newsitem .aspx?RecordID=11970*.

21. Thomas Hartung, "Food for Thought Look Back in Anger—What Clinical Studies Tell Us about Preclinical Work," *ALTEX* 30.3

(2013): 275–91; *www.ncbi.nlm.nih.gov/pmc/articles/PMC3790571/* (July 22, 2015).

22. "Animal Research FAQ," *American Association for Laboratory Animal Science*: *www.aalas.org/public-outreach/animal-research-faq* (May 28, 2015).

23. Ibid.

24. See *http://investigations.peta.org/nih-baby-monkey-experiments/*.

25. Aysha Akhtar, "Who Are the Animals in Animal Experiments?" *Huffington Post*, January 12, 2014, *www.huffingtonpost.com/aysha -akhtar/who-are-the-animals_b_4545611.html*.

26. Johnson, "More Suspicious Monkey Deaths."

27. Marc Bekoff, *Minding Animals: Awareness, Emotions, and Heart* (Oxford: Oxford University Press, 2002), 46.

28. I know this claim seems optimistic, but it's rooted in history. Evidence that the polio virus lived in the gastrointestinal tract in humans was ignored for decades because the popular theory, supported by experiments on monkeys, was that polio entered the body through the nose. Read all about it in the *Journal of Virology*. Hans J. Eggers, "Milestones in Early Poliomyelitis Research (1840 to 1949)," *Journal of Virology* 73.6 (1999): 4533–35. *www.ncbi.nlm.nih .gov/pmc/articles/PMC112492/* (July 17, 2015).

Chapter 7: Animals Used for Food and Clothing

1. You can read more about Ted and Leo here: "Ted and Leo: Starving Calves Rescued from Small Dairy," *FarmSanctuary.org*: *www.farm sanctuary.org/the-sanctuaries/rescued-animals/2013-rescues/ted-and-leo -starving-calves-rescued-from-small-dairy/* (May 28, 2015).

2. Chipotle is one example of this type of marketing: "On the Farm: Responsibly Raising the Bar," *Chipotle*: *http://chipotle.com/food-with -integrity?_ga=1.134854897.1853803046.1432829267* (May 28, 2015).

3. "Livestock and Meat Domestic Data," *United States Department of Agriculture*, last updated October 28, 2015, *http://ers.usda.gov/data -products/livestock-meat-domestic-data.aspx#26063*.

4. National Oceanic and Atmospheric Administration, "Fisheries of the United States, 2012," *US Department of Commerce*: *www.st.nmfs.noaa. gov/Assets/commercial/fus/fus12/FUS_2012_factsheet.pdf* (May 27, 2015).

5. "Red Meat and Poultry Production," *USDA*, last updated April 28,

2015, *http://ers.usda.gov/datafiles/Livestock_Meat_Domestic_Data/Meat_ statistics/Red_meat_and_poultry_production/RedMeatPoultry_ProdFull.pdf*.

6. That's not a typo. Farm and slaughterhouse workers have repeatedly been caught on camera putting foreign objects into the genitals of female animals, having sex with animals, or pretending to. More information can be found at *www.peta.org/videos/sexual-deviance-and -sexual-abuse-of-animals-factory-farmings-dirty-little-secret/* and *www.peta .org/blog/sexual-abuse-animals-recurring-theme-factory-farms/*.

7. Elizabeth R. Rumley, "States' Farm Animal Confinement Statutes," *National Agricultural Law Center*: *http://nationalaglawcenter .org/state-compilations/farm-animal-welfare/* (May 27, 2015).

8. Cassandra Brooks, "Consequences of Increased Global Meat Consumption on the Global Environment—Trade in Virtual Water, Energy and Nutrients," *StanfordWoods Institute for the Environment*: *https://woods.stanford.edu/environmental-venture-projects/consequences -increased-global-meat-consumption-global-environment* (May 27, 2015).

9. Thomas C. Frohlich, "States Killing the Most Animals for Food," *USA Today*, April 15, 2015, *www.usatoday.com/story/money/ business/2015/04/15/247-wall-st-states-killing-animals/25807125/*.

10. "Sow Housing," *National Pork Producers Council*: *www.nppc.org/issues/ animal-health-safety/sow-housing/* (May 27, 2015).

11. "Welfare Implications of Gestation Sow Housing: Literature Review," *American Veterinary Medical Association (AVMA)*, January 31, 2014, *www.avma.org/KB/Resources/LiteratureReviews/Pages/Welfare -Implications-of-Gestation-Sow-Housing.aspx*.

12. Gail Golab, "Making Difficult Welfare Choices—Housing for Pregnant Sows," *AVMA*, May 18, 2012, *http://atwork.avma.org/2012/ 05/18/making-difficult-welfare-choices-housing-for-pregnant-sows/*.

13. "Bird Welfare Positions Modified," *AVMA News*, January 1, 2002, *www.avma.org/News/JAVMANews/Pages/s011502m.aspx*.

14. National Agricultural Law Center, "States' Farm Animals Welfare Statutes: State of Michigan" (Agricultural Law Research Project, University of Arkansas, n.d.), *http://nationalaglawcenter.org/wp-content/ uploads/assets/farmanimal/michigan.pdf* (May 28, 2015).

15. "Welfare Implications of Laying Hen Housing: Literature Review," *AVMA*, January 26, 2012, *www.avma.org/KB/Resources/ LiteratureReviews/Pages/Welfare-Implications-of-Laying-Hen-Housing.aspx*.

16. "Welfare Implications of Dehorning and Disbudding Cattle:

Literature Review," *AVMA*, July 15, 2014, *www.avma.org/KB/ Resources/LiteratureReviews/Pages/Welfare-Implications-of-Dehorning -and-Disbudding-Cattle.aspx*.

17. "Welfare Implications of Castration of Cattle: Literature Review," *AVMA*, July 15, 2014, *www.avma.org/KB/Resources/LiteratureReviews/ Pages/castration-cattle-bgnd.aspx*, and "Welfare Implications of Swine Castration: Literature Review," *AVMA*, May 25, 2013, *www.avma .org/KB/Resources/LiteratureReviews/Pages/Welfare-Implications-of -Swine-Castration.aspx*.

18. Ibid. See also the short documentary *Meet Your Meat*, at *Meat. org*. The AVMA documents listed in the previous notes contain a wealth of information on these practices. It confounds me that the AVMA can point out that certain practices cause enormous pain and suffering, but fail to condemn those same practices.

19. "Welfare Implications of Beak Trimming: Literature Review," *AVMA*, February 7, 2010, *www.avma.org/KB/Resources/Literature Reviews/Pages/beak-trimming-bgnd.aspx*.

20. "Bird Welfare Positions Modified," *JAVMA News*, January 1, 2002, *www.avma.org/News/JAVMANews/Pages/s011502m.aspx*.

21. "Background: Farm Milk Production," *USDA*: *www.ers.usda.gov/ topics/animal-products/dairy/background.aspx* (May 28, 2015).

22. Ibid.

23. Joe Vansickle, "Goal: Producing More Quality Pigs," *National Hog Farmer*, June 15, 2009, *http://nationalhogfarmer.com/health-diseases/ 0615-producing-quality-pigs*.

24. Ibid.

25. Dale Miller, "Flirting with 30 Pigs/Mated Female/Year Goal," *National Hog Farmer*, September 19, 2011, *http://nationalhogfarmer .com/genetics-reproduction/30pigs-mated-female-year-0919*.

26. S. F. Bilgili, "Recent Advances in Electrical Stunning," *Poultry Science* 78, no. 2 (1999): 282–86.

27. "Slaughter Inspection 101," *USDA*, last updated August 9, 2013, *www.fsis.usda.gov/wps/portal/fsis/topics/food-safety-education/get-answers/ food-safety-fact-sheets/production-and-inspection/slaughter-inspection-101/ slaughter-inspection-101*.

28. Casey Toner, "Poultry Inspections to Undergo Sweeping Change in Food Inspections," *Alabama Local News*, March 17, 2015, *www.al .com/news/index.ssf/2015/03/chicken_plants_to_replace_fede.html*.

29. Helen Bottemiller, "House Panel Debates New Poultry Inspection Rule," *Food Safety News*, March 9, 2012, *www.foodsafetynews.com/2012/03/house-panel-debates-merits-of-new-poultry-inspection-rule/#.VPN9tS7wFZ8*.

30. FAO Newsroom, "Livestock a Major Threat to Environment: Remedies Urgently Needed," *Food and Agriculture Organization of the United Nations*, November 29, 2006, *www.fao.org/newsroom/en/News/2006/1000448/index.html*.

31. Katherine Boehrer, "This Is How Much Water It Takes to Make Your Favorite Foods," *Huffington Post*, October 13, 2014, *www.huffingtonpost.com/2014/10/13/food-water-footprint_n_5952862.html*.

32. Mario Herrero et al., "Biomass Use, Production, Feed Efficiencies, and Greenhouse Gas Emissions from Global Livestock Systems," *Proceedings of the National Academy of Sciences of the United States of America* 110, no. 52 (December 2013): 20888–893; doi: 10.1073/pnas.1308149110.

33. Bryan Walsh, "The Triple Whopper Environmental Impact of Global Meet Production," *Time*, http://science.time.com/2013/12/16/the-triple-whopper-environmental-impact-of-global-meat-production/ (December 13, 2015). For this and a number of other reasons, I do not support programs that donate cows and other large animals to impoverished nations in which the land is not suitable to support their heft and nutritional needs. Stories abound of these animals only further impoverishing the families who receive them, as they try desperately to feed the cow enough to survive, much less produce milk, and attempt to prevent the inevitable soil degradation that results when the soil is trampled and denuded by a large animal.

34. Ibid.

35. Center for a Livable Future, "Health and Environmental Implications of US Meat Consumption and Production," *Johns Hopkins Bloomburg School of Public Health*: *www.jhsph.edu/research/centers-and-institutes/johns-hopkins-center-for-a-livable-future/projects/meatless_monday/resources/meat_consumption.html* (May 29, 2015).

36. Brooks, "Consequences of Increased Global Meat Consumption."

37. Center for a Livable Future, "Health and Environmental Implications."

38. Ibid.

39. If you have the stomach for it, read Andrew Tarantola, "How Leather Is Slowly Killing the People and Places That Make It," *http://gizmodo .com/how-leather-is-slowly-killing-the-people-and-places-tha-1572678618.*

40. Bryan Walsh, "Environmental Groups Sue the FDA over Antibiotics and Meat Production," *Time Magazine*, March 25, 2011, *http://science.time.com/2011/05/25/environmental-groups-sue-the-fda-over -antibiotics-and-meat-production/.*

41. Center for a Livable Future, "Health and Environmental Implications."

42. Bryan Walsh, "Meat and Antibiotics: Getting Our Animals Off Drugs," *Time Magazine*, June 29, 2010, *http://science.time.com/2010/ 06/29/meat-and-antibiotics-getting-our-animals-off-drugs/.*

43. FAO Newsroom, "Cattle Ranching Is Encroaching on Forests in Latin America," *Food and Agriculture Organization of the United Nations*, June 8, 2005, *www.fao.org/newsroom/en/news/2005/102924/.*

44. "Livestock and the Environment," *Food and Agriculture Organization of the United Nations: www.fao.org/livestock-environment/en/* (May 29, 2015).

45. Lesley A. Peterson, "Detailed Discussion of Fur Animals and Fur Production" (paper, Animal Legal and Historical Center, Michigan State University College of Law, 2010), *www.animallaw.info/article/ detailed-discussion-fur-animals-and-fur-production.*

46. "The Fur Farm Fallacy," *Animal Issues* 34, no. 3 (Fall 2003), cited in "Get the Facts," *BornFreeUSA.org: www.bornfreeusa.org/facts.php? p=372&more=1.*

47. "Sheep Shearing: Exposed on Shearing Day," *Ranching with Sheep: www.ranching-with-sheep.com/sheep-shearing.html* (May 29, 2015).

48. "Shearing," *Sheep 201: A Beginner's Guide to Raising Sheep: www .sheep101.info/201/shearing.html* (May 29, 2015).

49. Anna Schechter, "PETA: There's No Such Thing as Humane Wool," *NBCNews.com*, http://www.nbcnews.com/news/ investigations/peta-theres-no-such-thing-humane-wool-n151326 (December 15, 2015).

50. Miroslav Volf, *Exclusion and Embrace* (Nashville: Abingdon, 1996), 66.

51. Andrew Linzey and Priscilla N. Cohn, "Blind Spot," *Journal of Animal Ethics* 5, no. 1 (Spring 2015): v–vi, *http://www.jstor.org/ stable/10.5406/janimalethics.5.1.v.*